AF483539

ETTA'S ENCHANTING ANIMALS

A–Z WITH GRANDMA AND ME

ILLUSTRATED BY ETTA ANDERSON
AND LOIS FICK

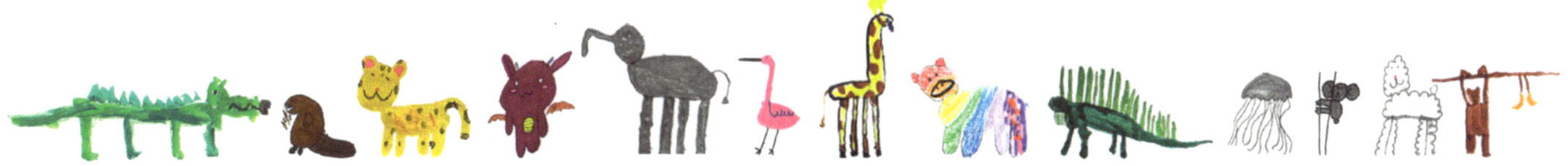

First Edition
ISBN: 9798851190438 (Hardcover)

Printed and distributed by IngramSpark.com

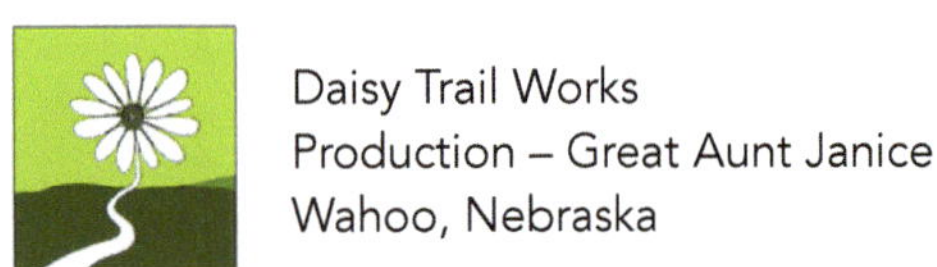

Daisy Trail Works
Production – Great Aunt Janice
Wahoo, Nebraska

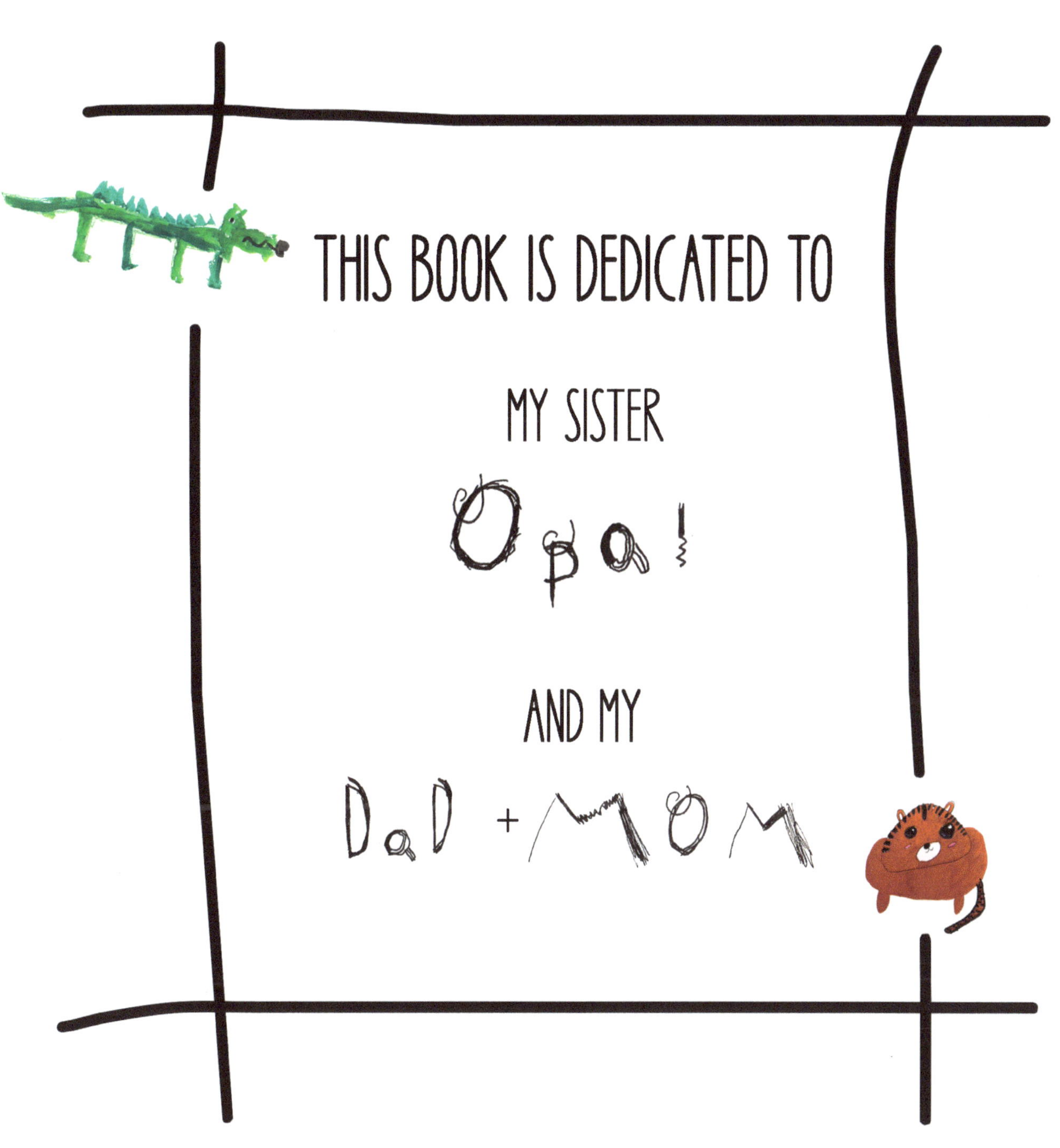

THIS BOOK IS DEDICATED TO
MY SISTER
Opal!
AND MY
DaD + MOM

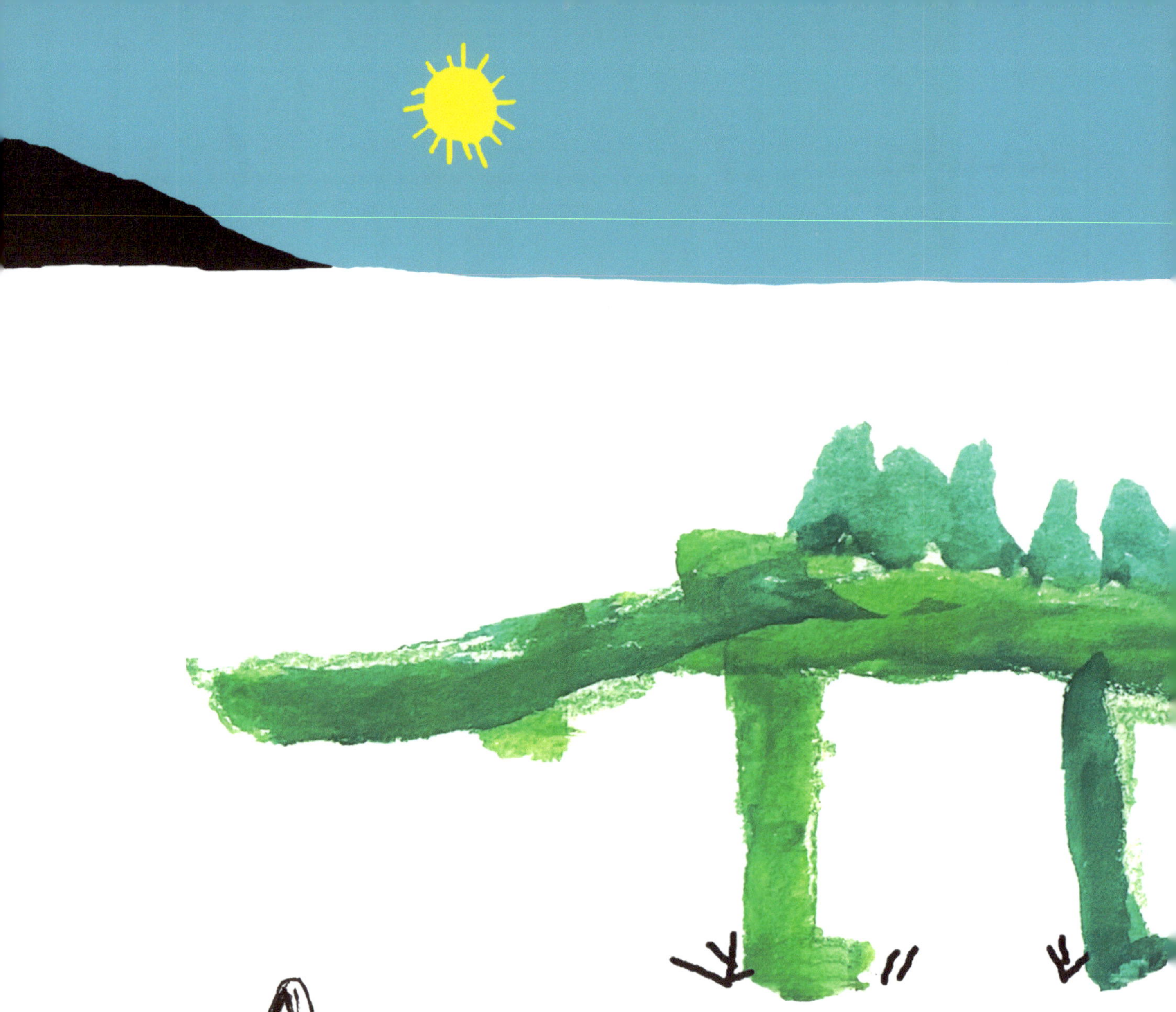

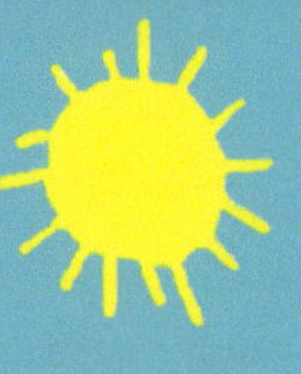

A IS FOR ALLIGATOR

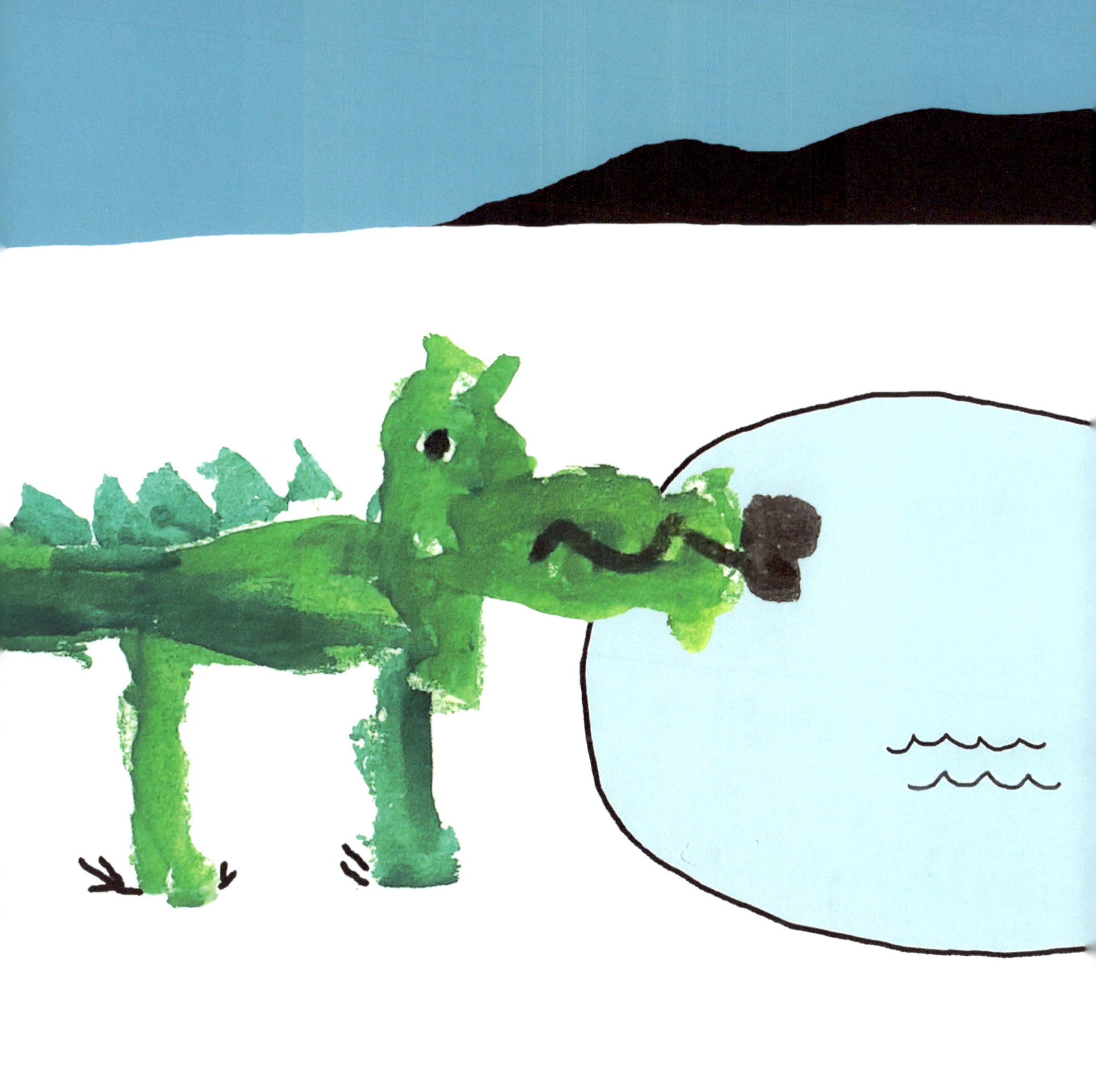

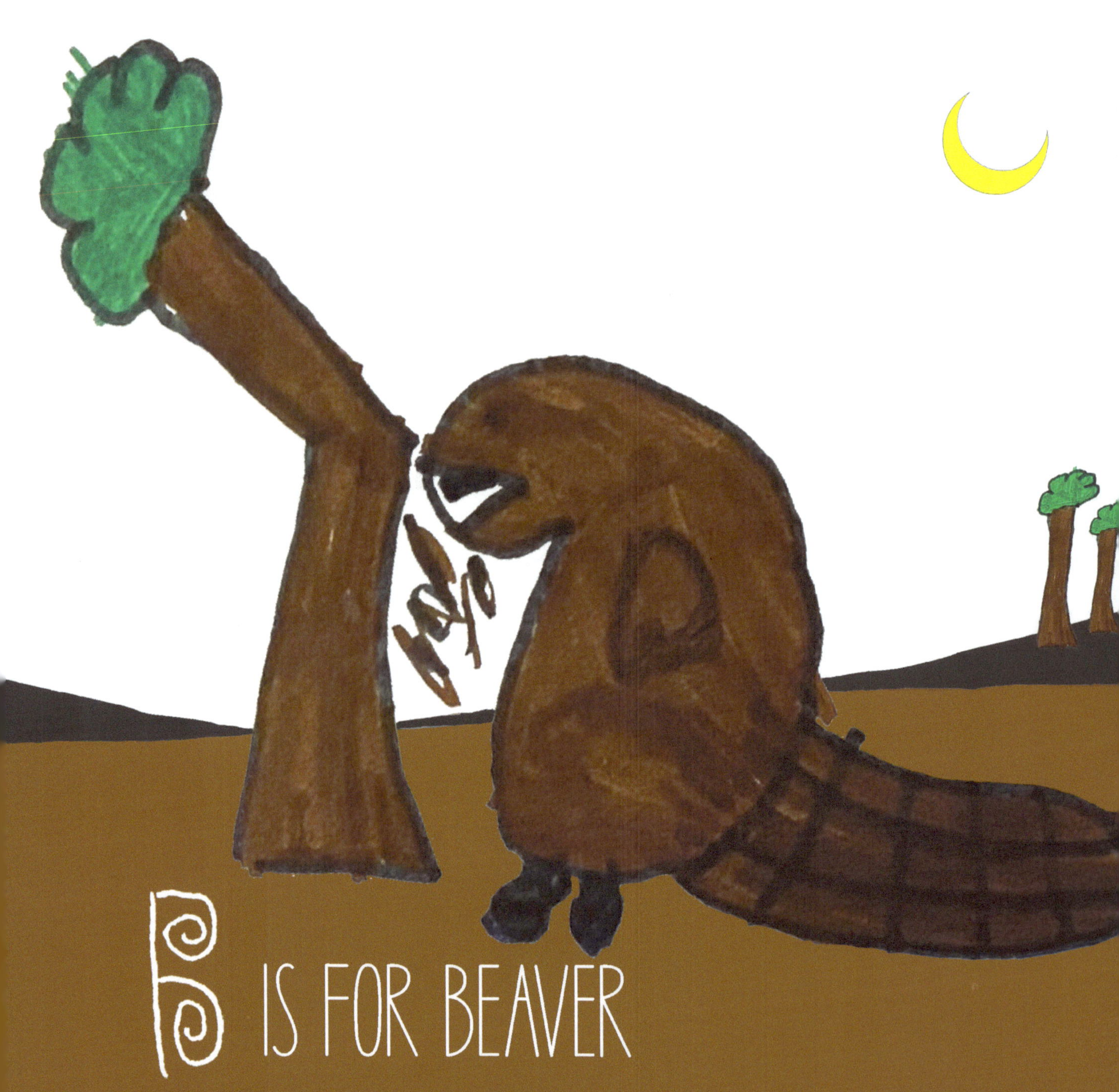
B IS FOR BEAVER

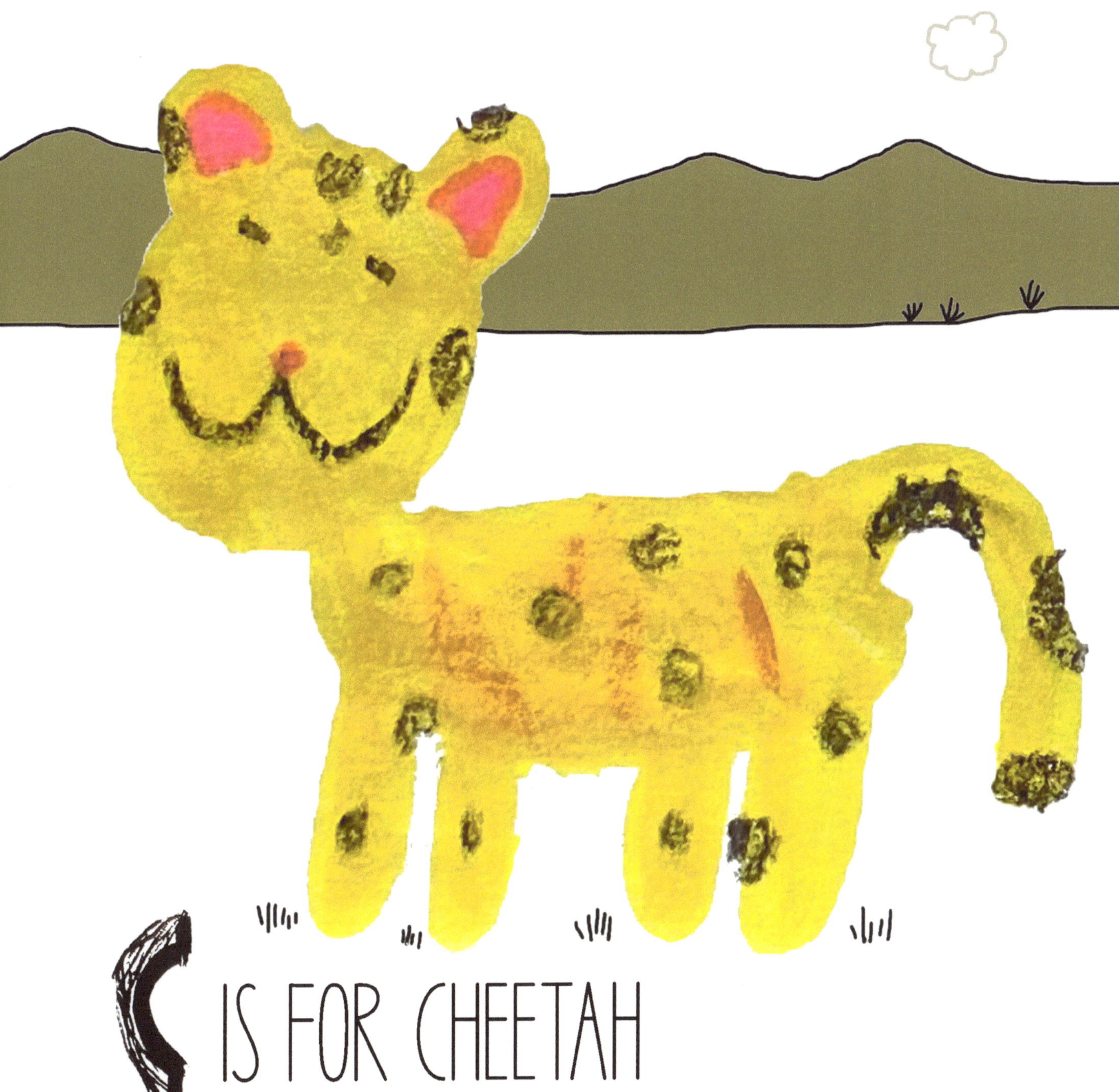

IS FOR CHEETAH

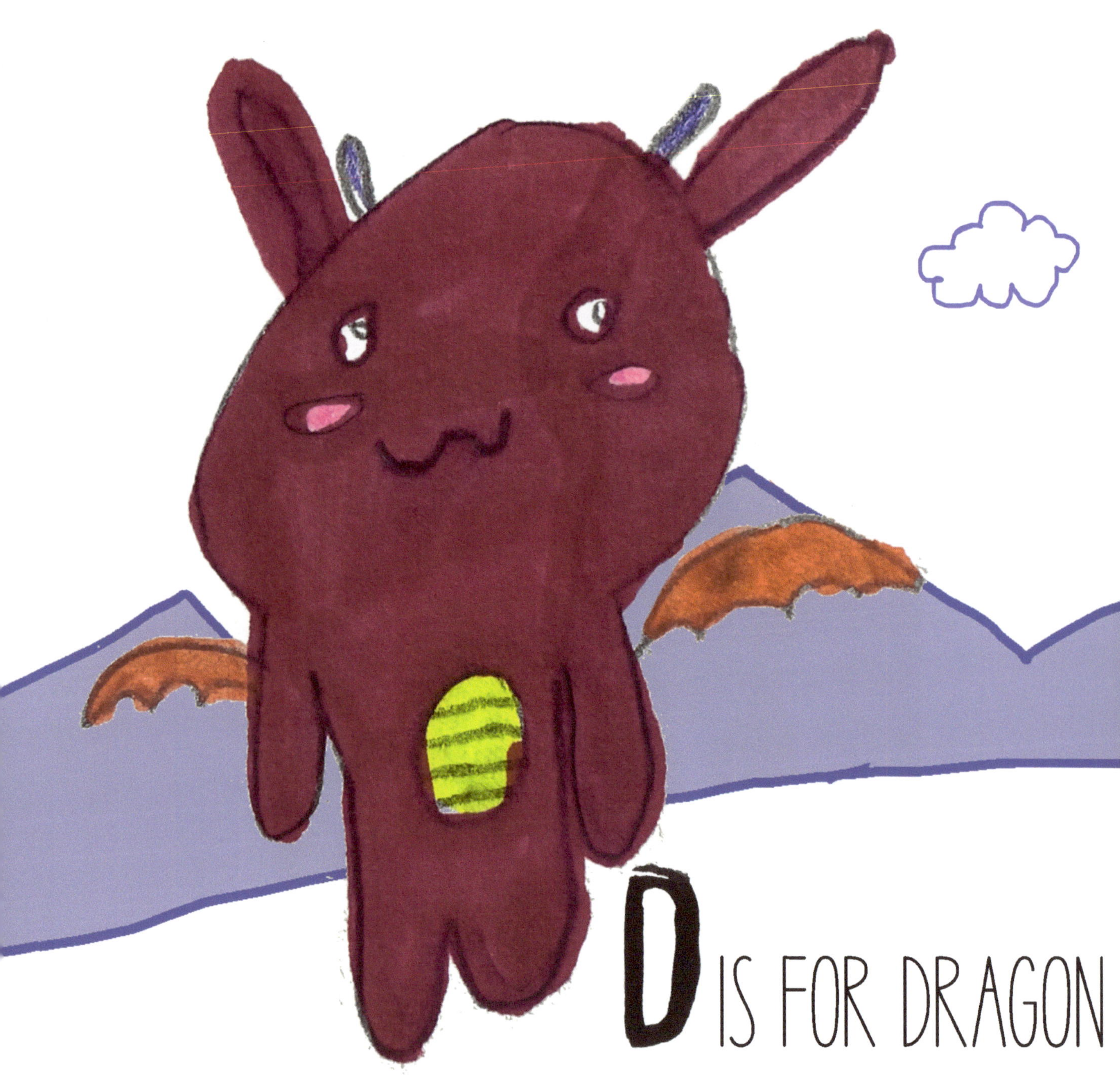
D IS FOR DRAGON

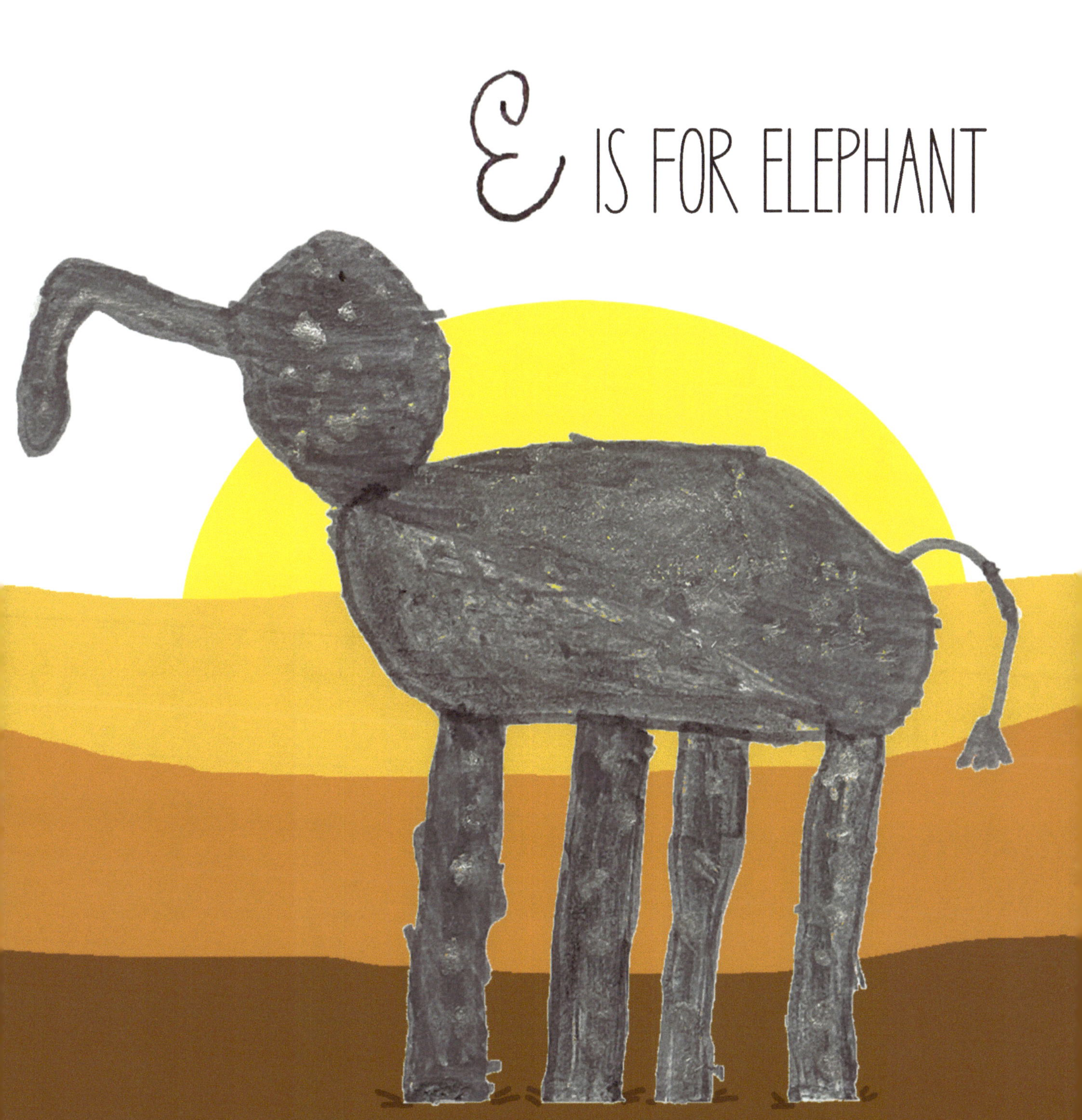

E IS FOR ELEPHANT

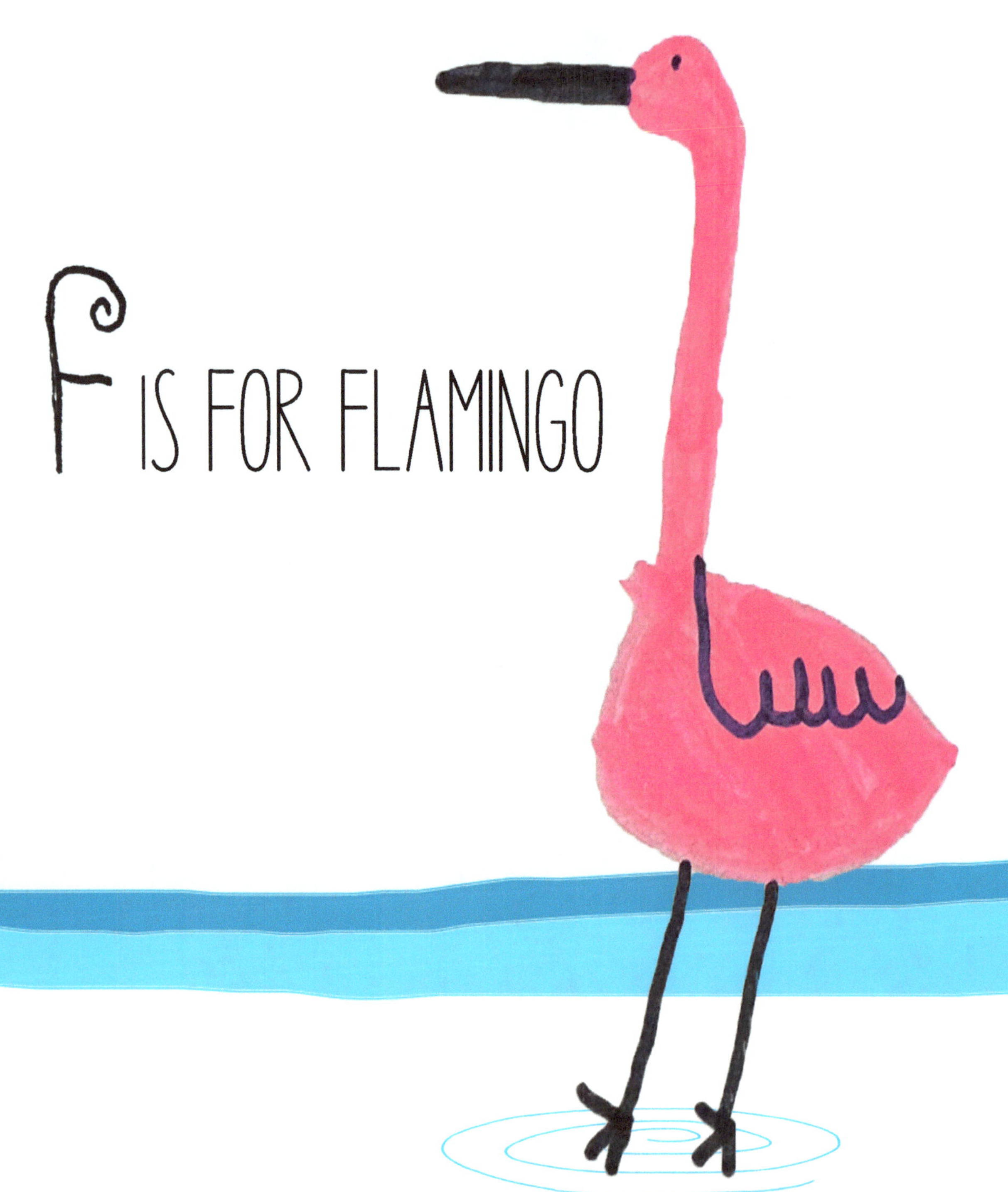

F IS FOR FLAMINGO

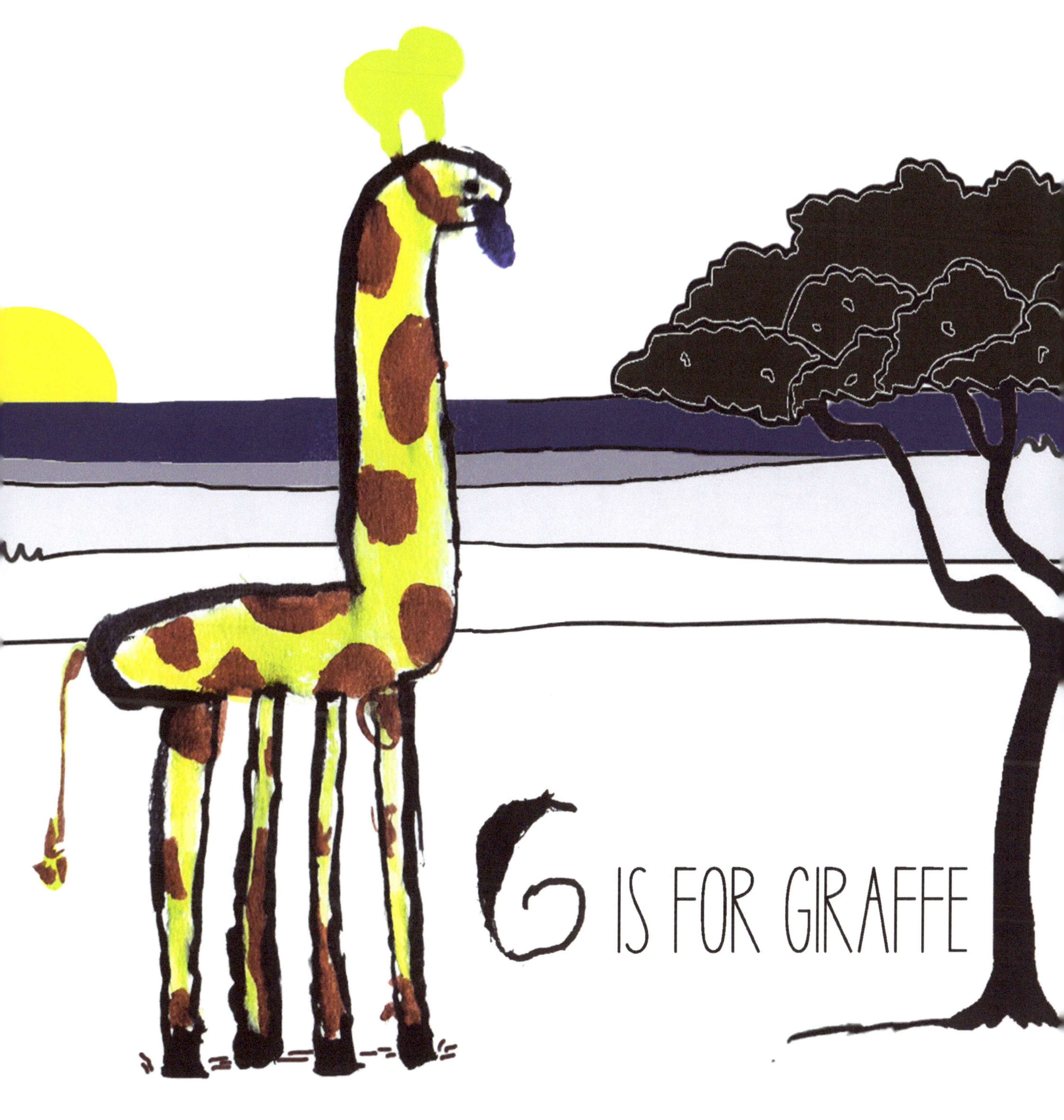

G IS FOR GIRAFFE

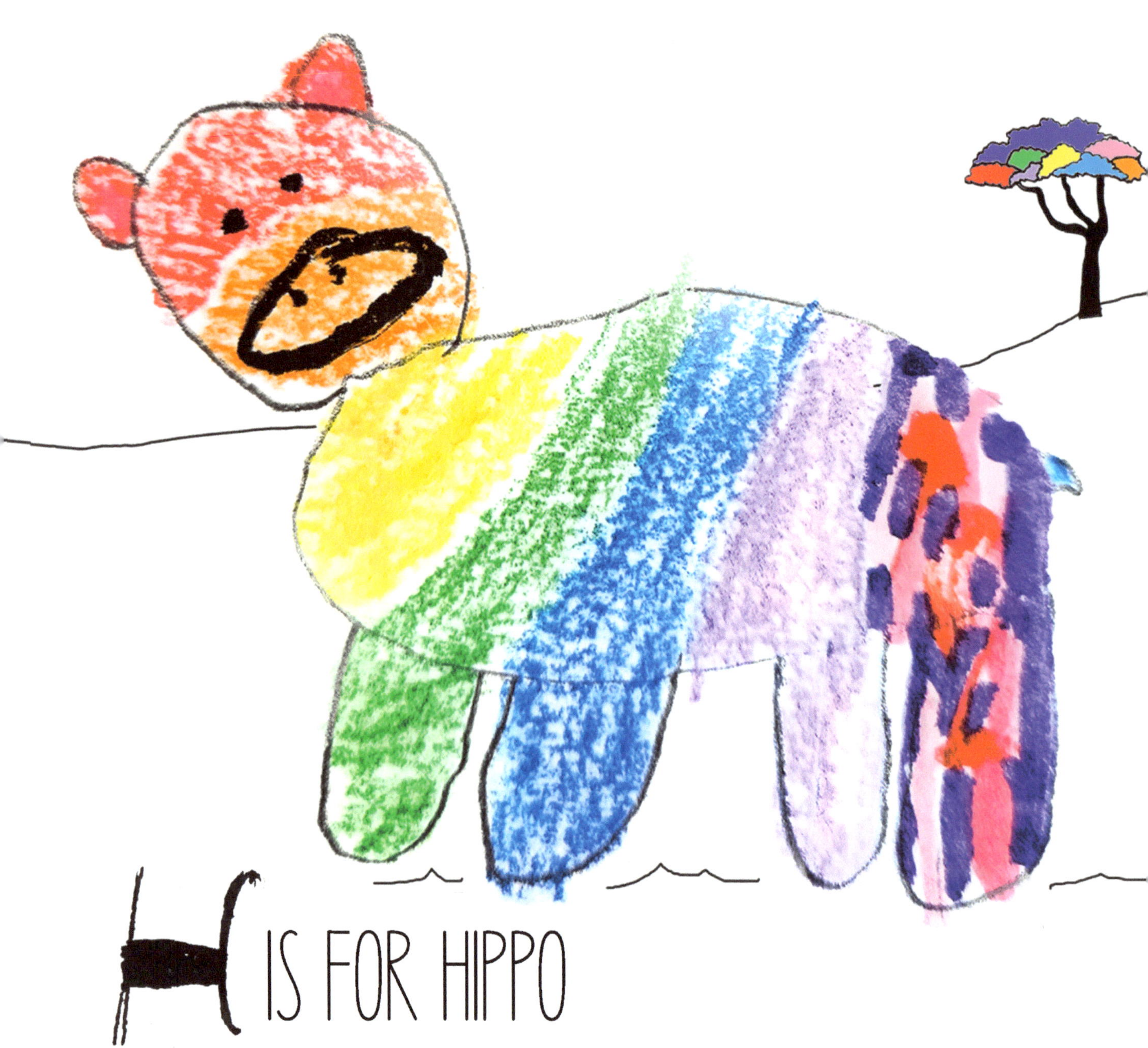
H IS FOR HIPPO

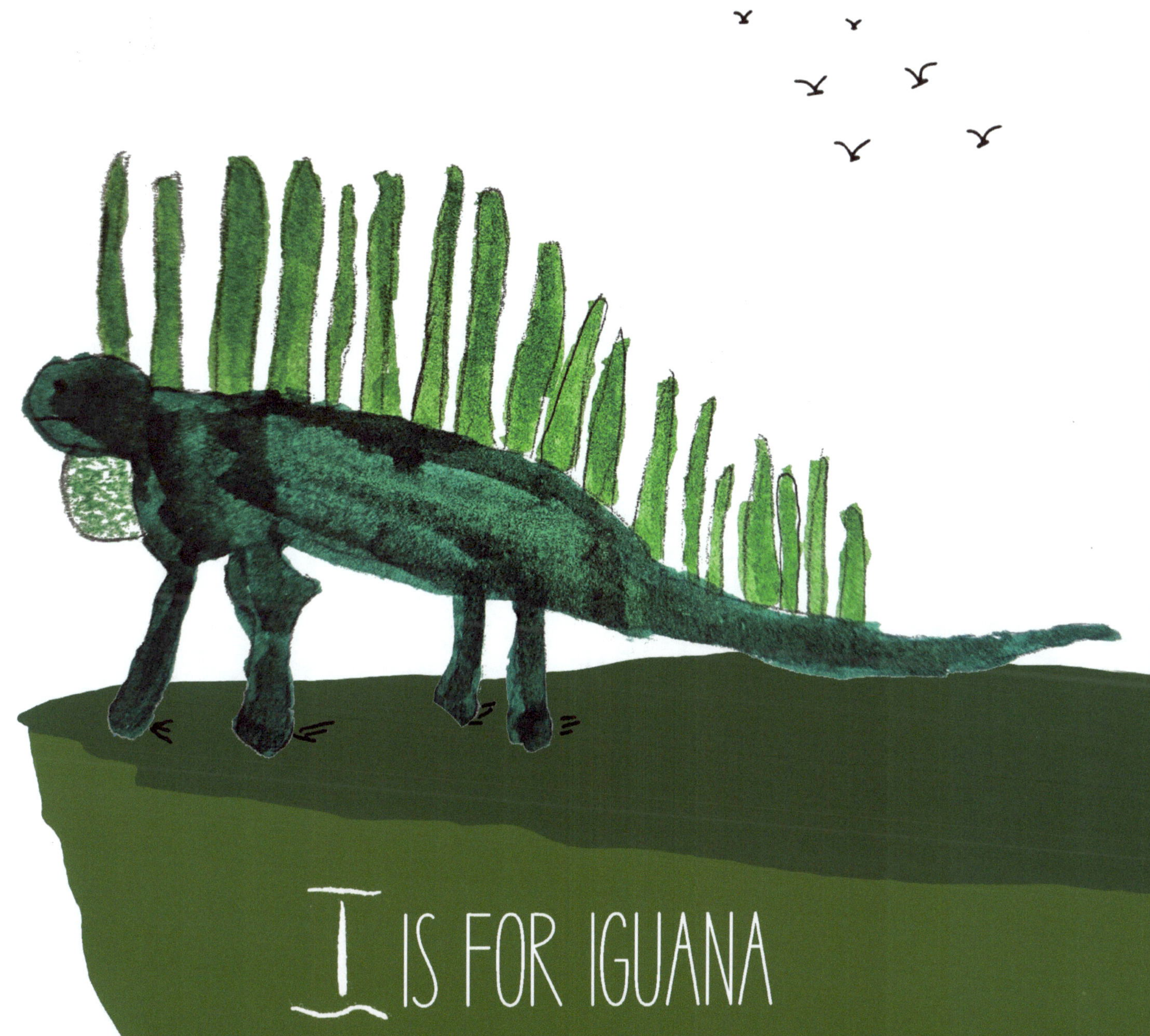
I IS FOR IGUANA

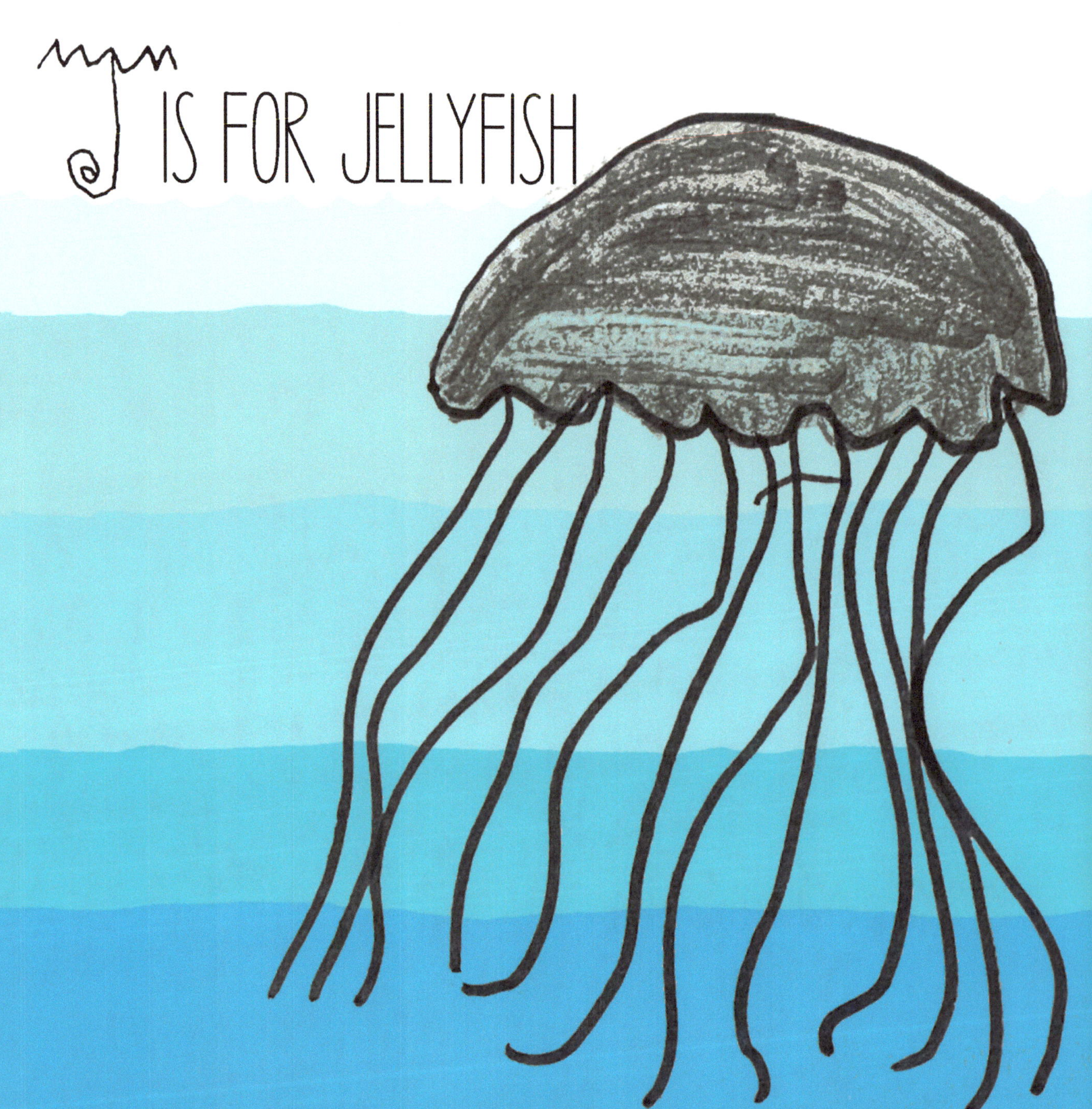

J IS FOR JELLYFISH

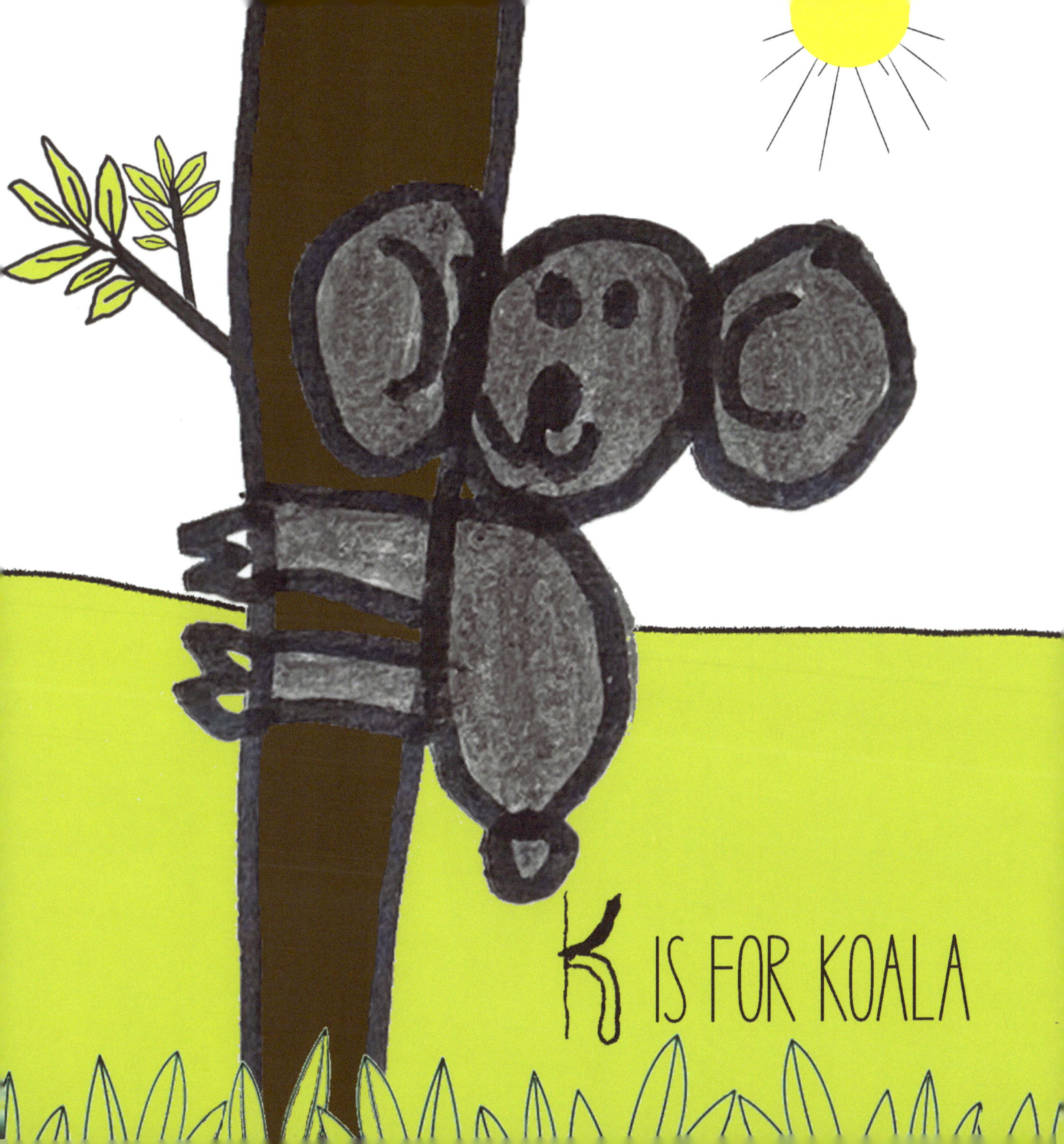
K IS FOR KOALA

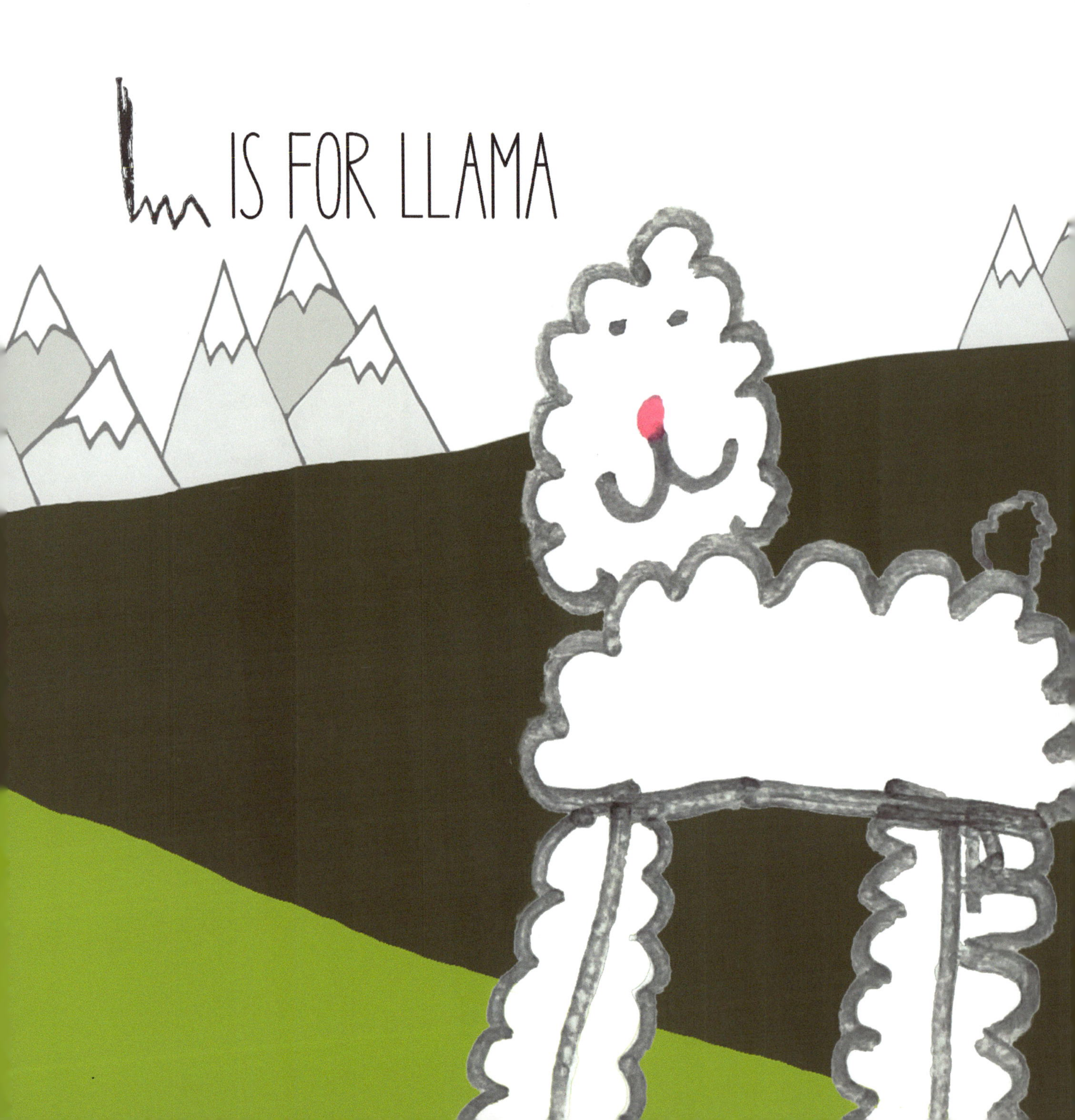
IS FOR LLAMA

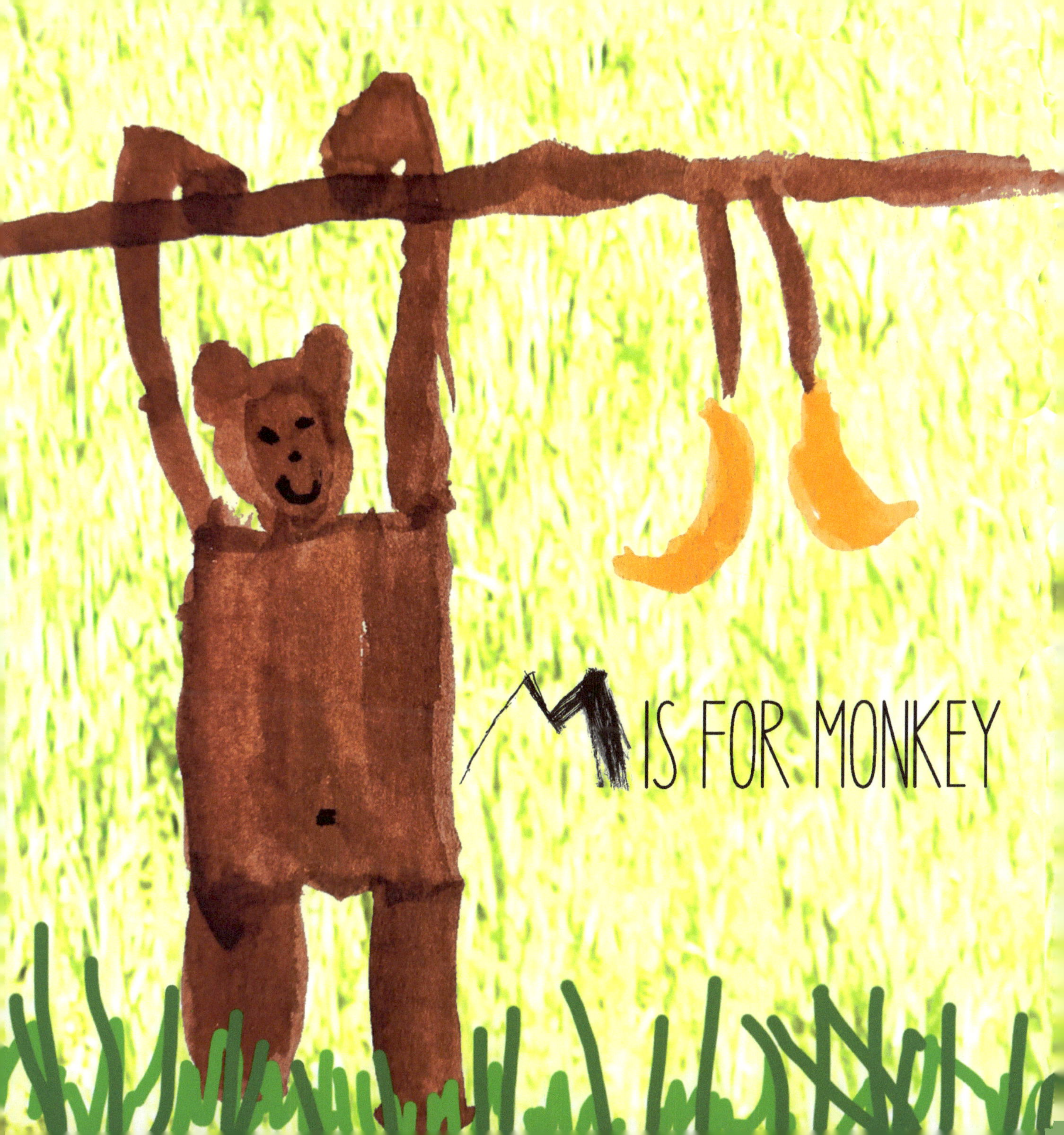

M IS FOR MONKEY

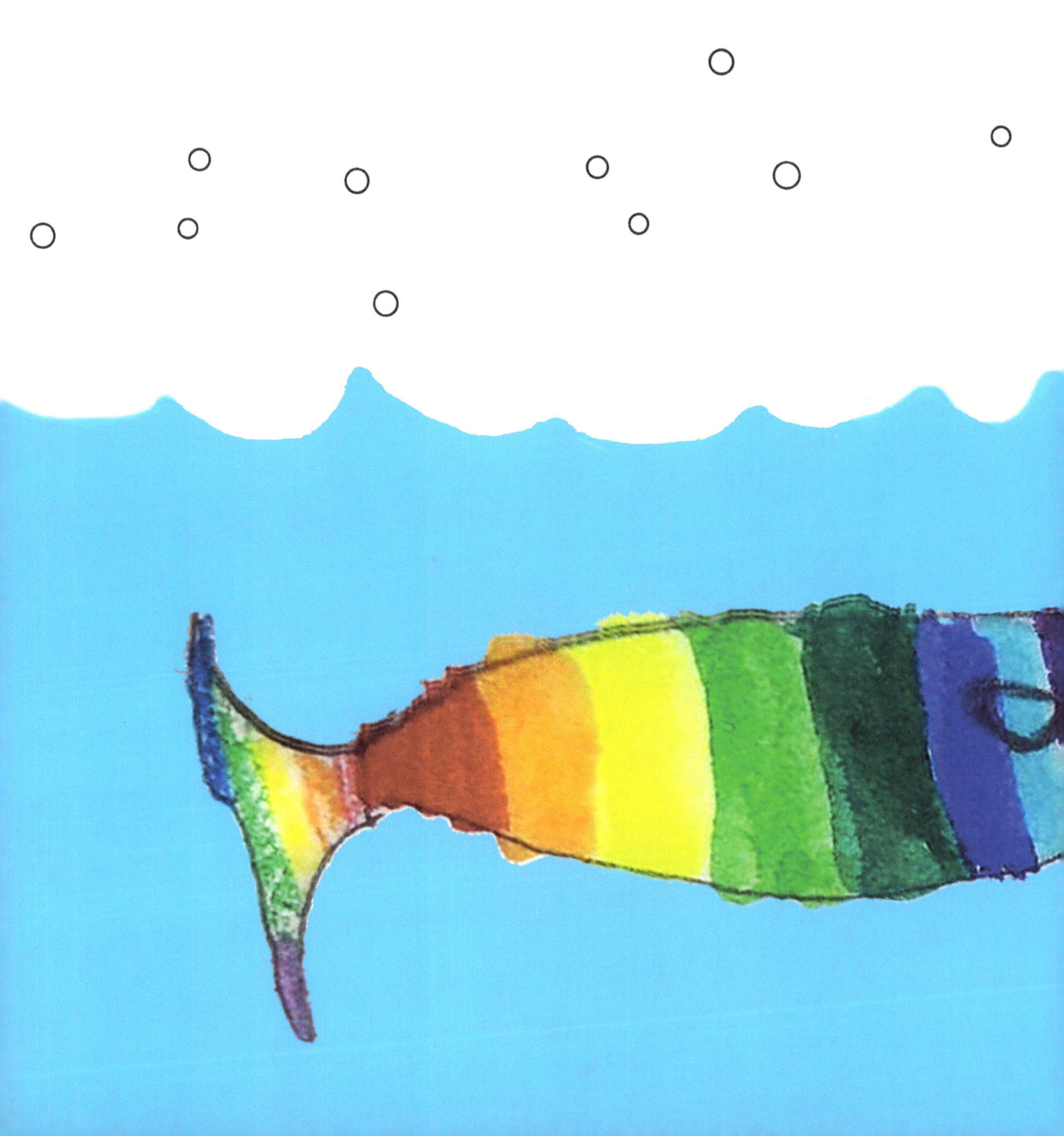

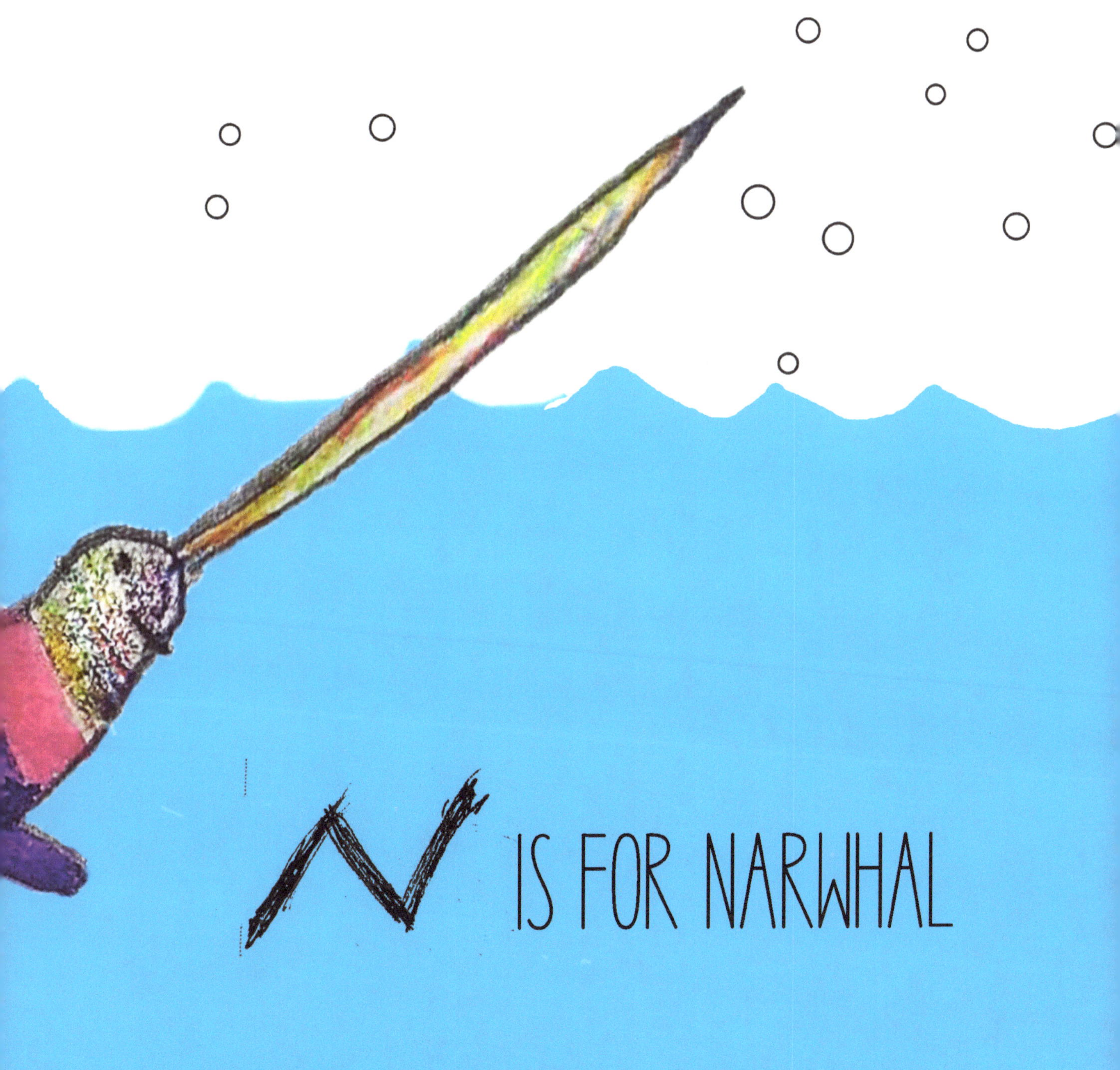
N IS FOR NARWHAL

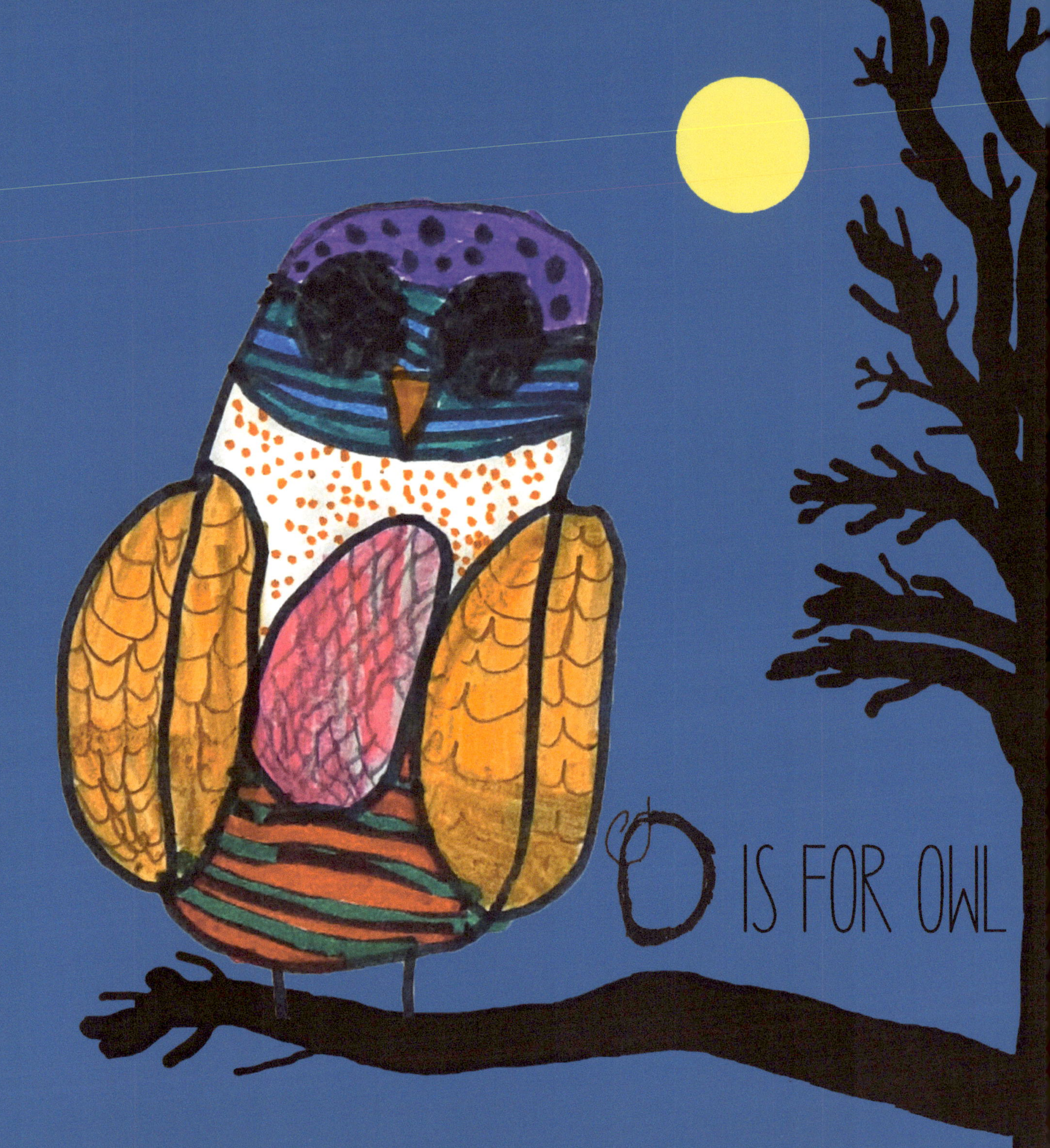

O IS FOR OWL

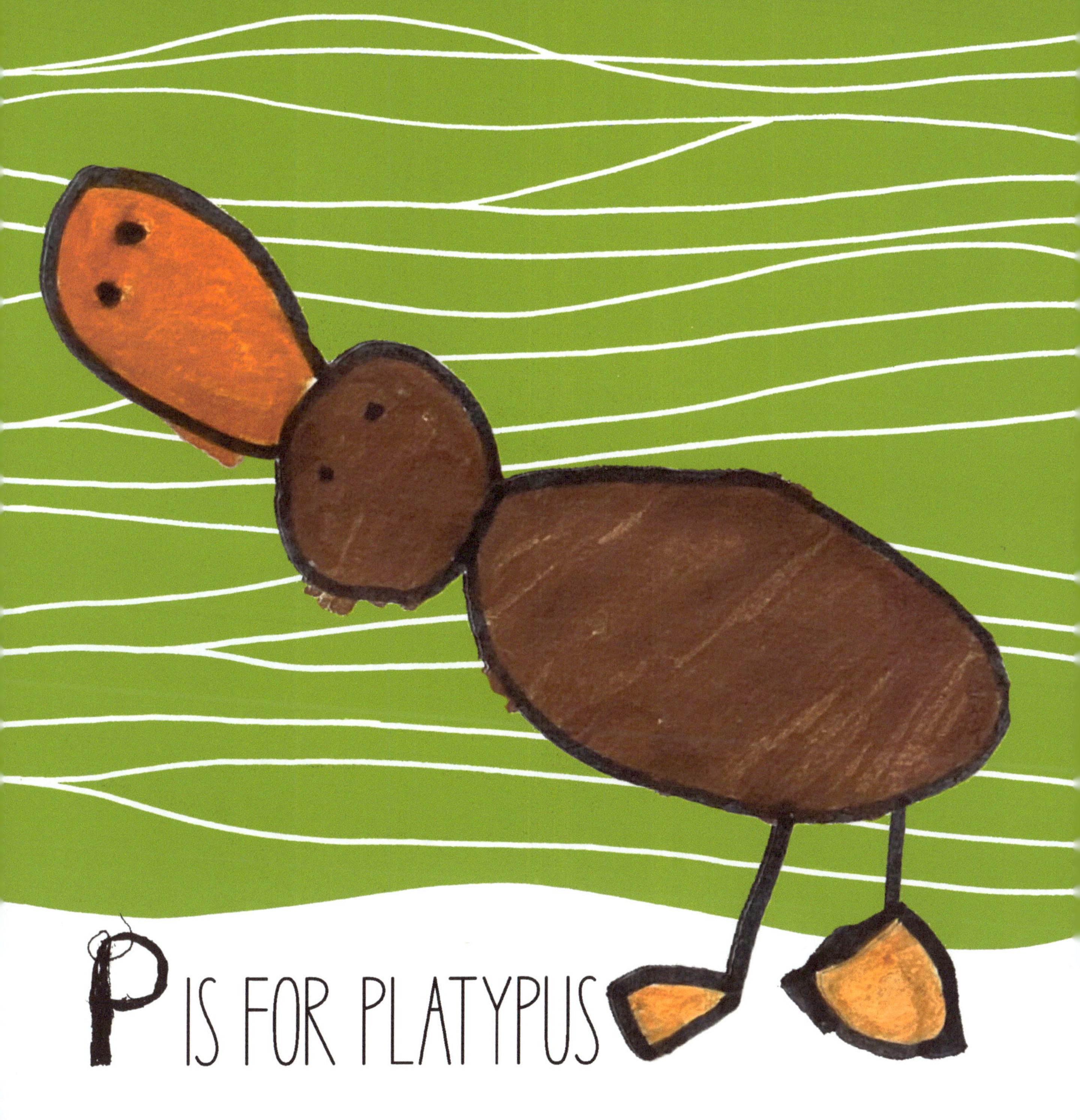
P IS FOR PLATYPUS

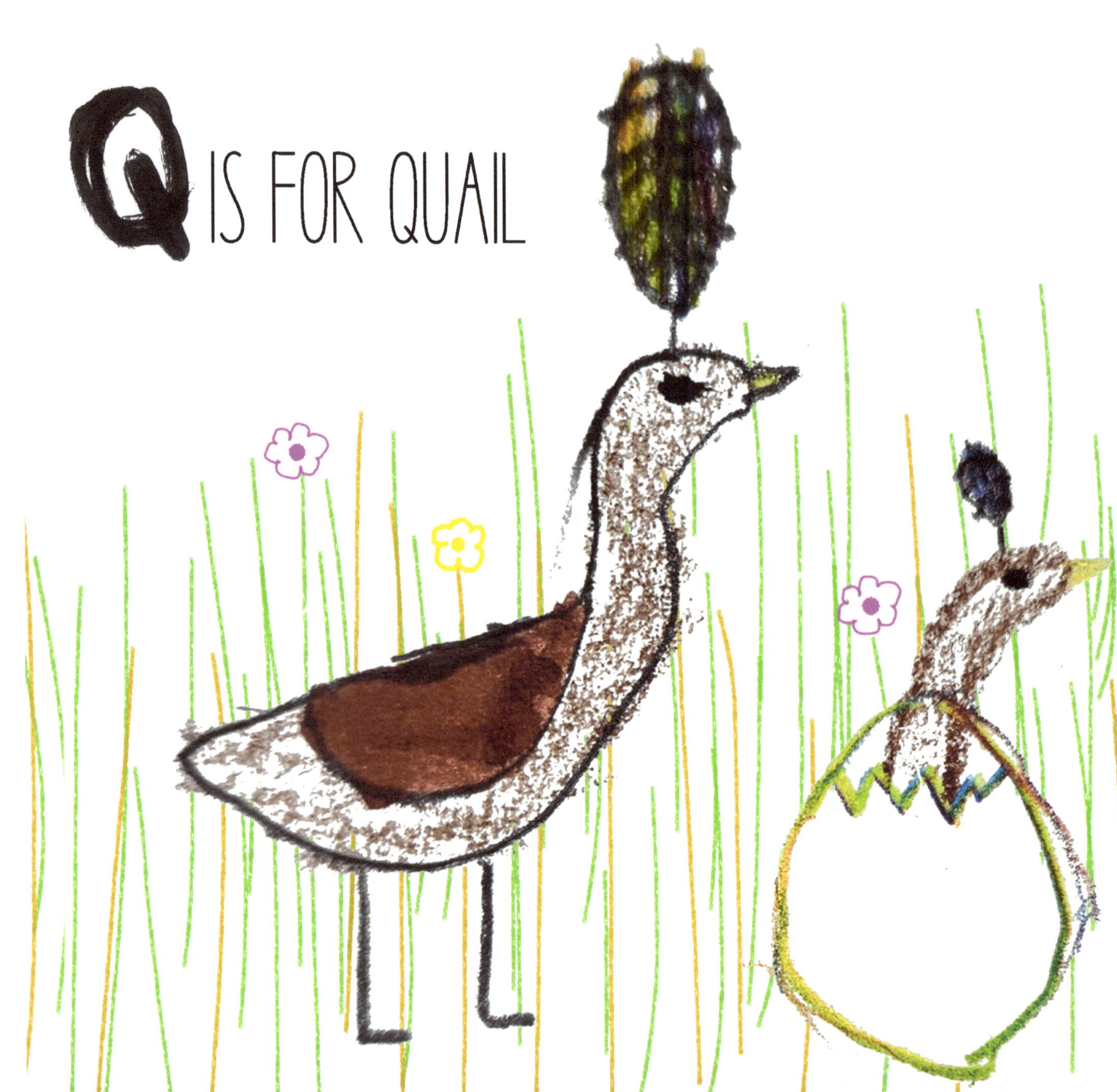
Q IS FOR QUAIL

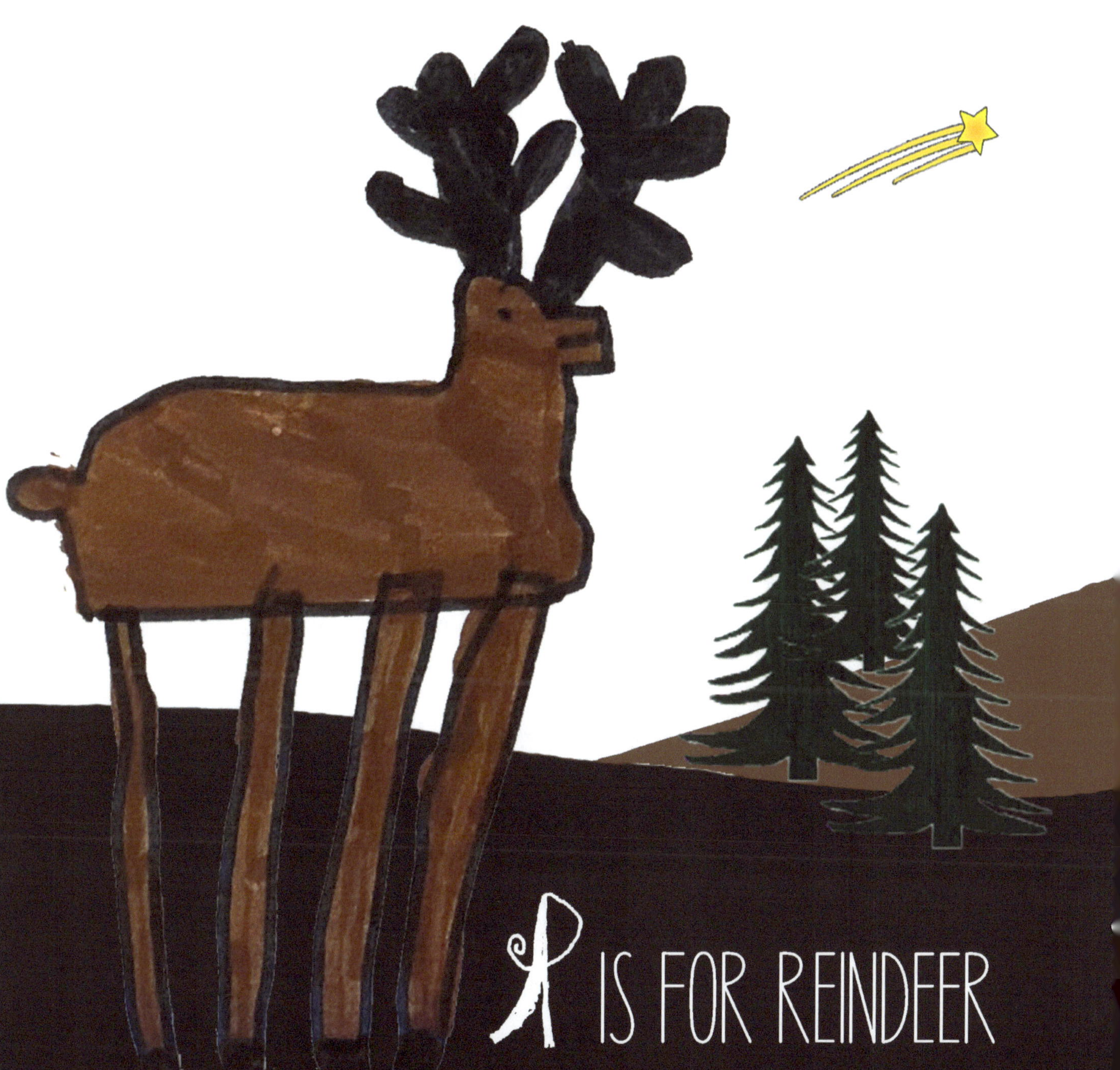
R IS FOR REINDEER

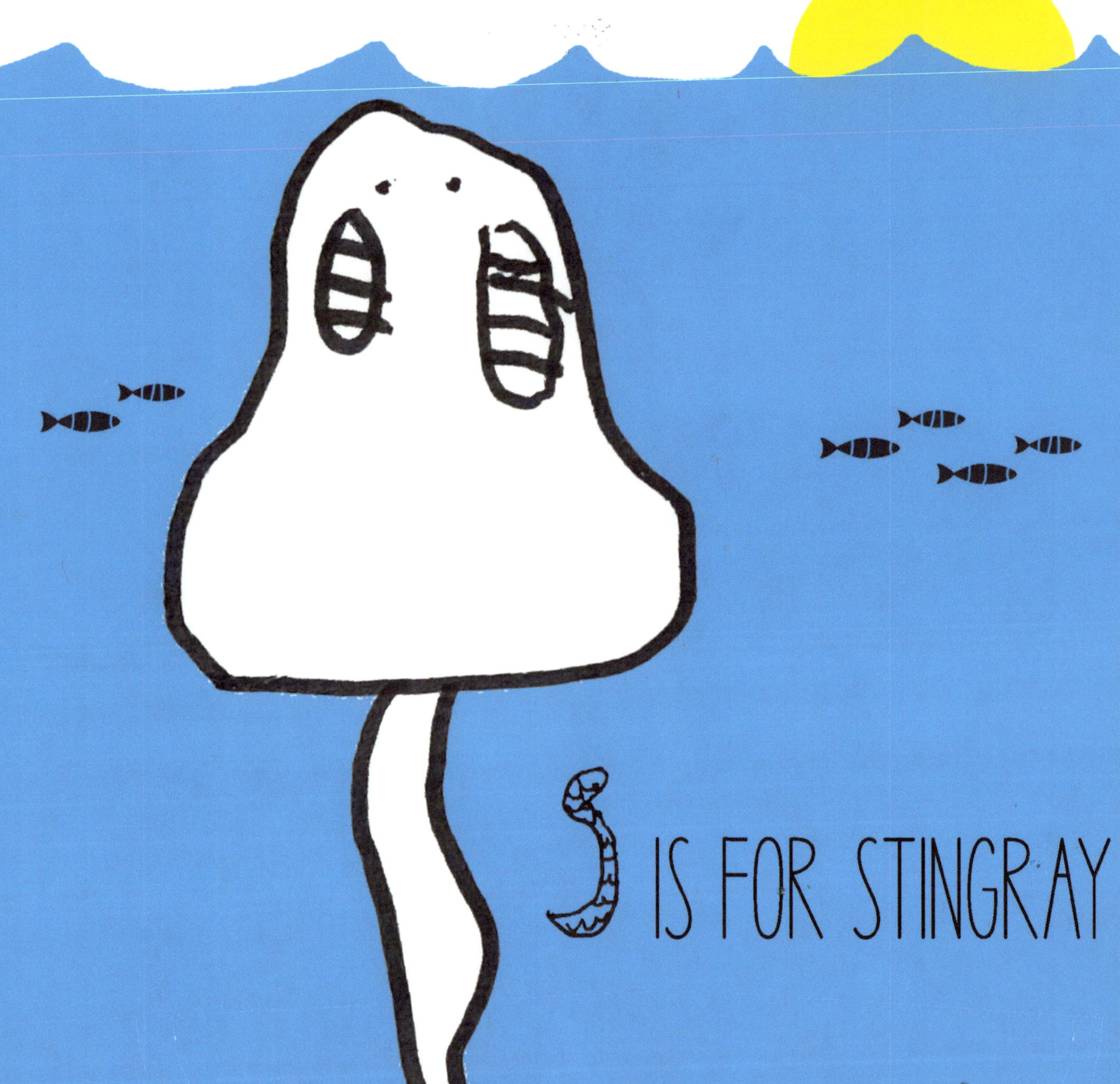

S IS FOR STINGRAY

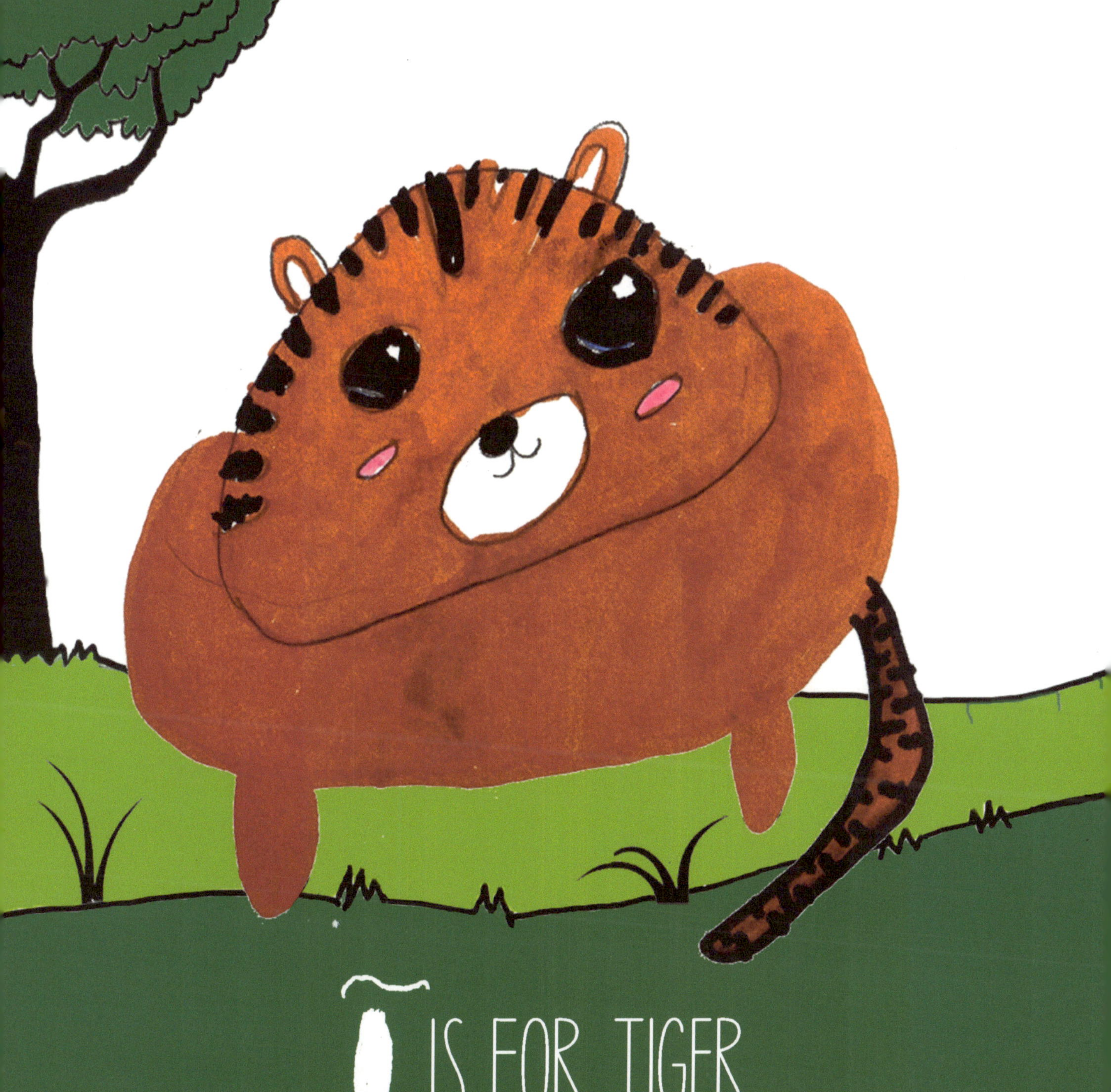

T IS FOR TIGER

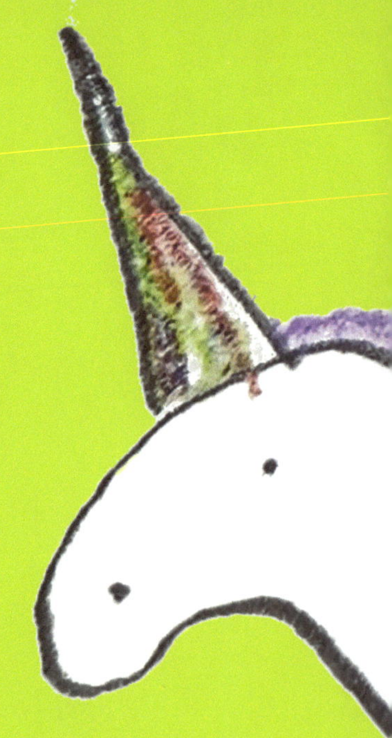
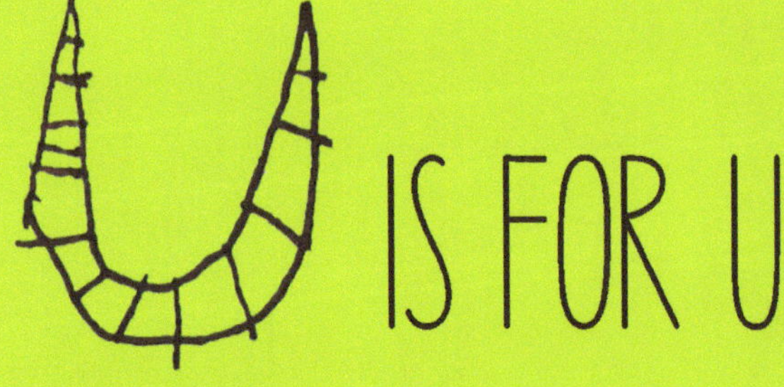

U IS FOR UNICORN

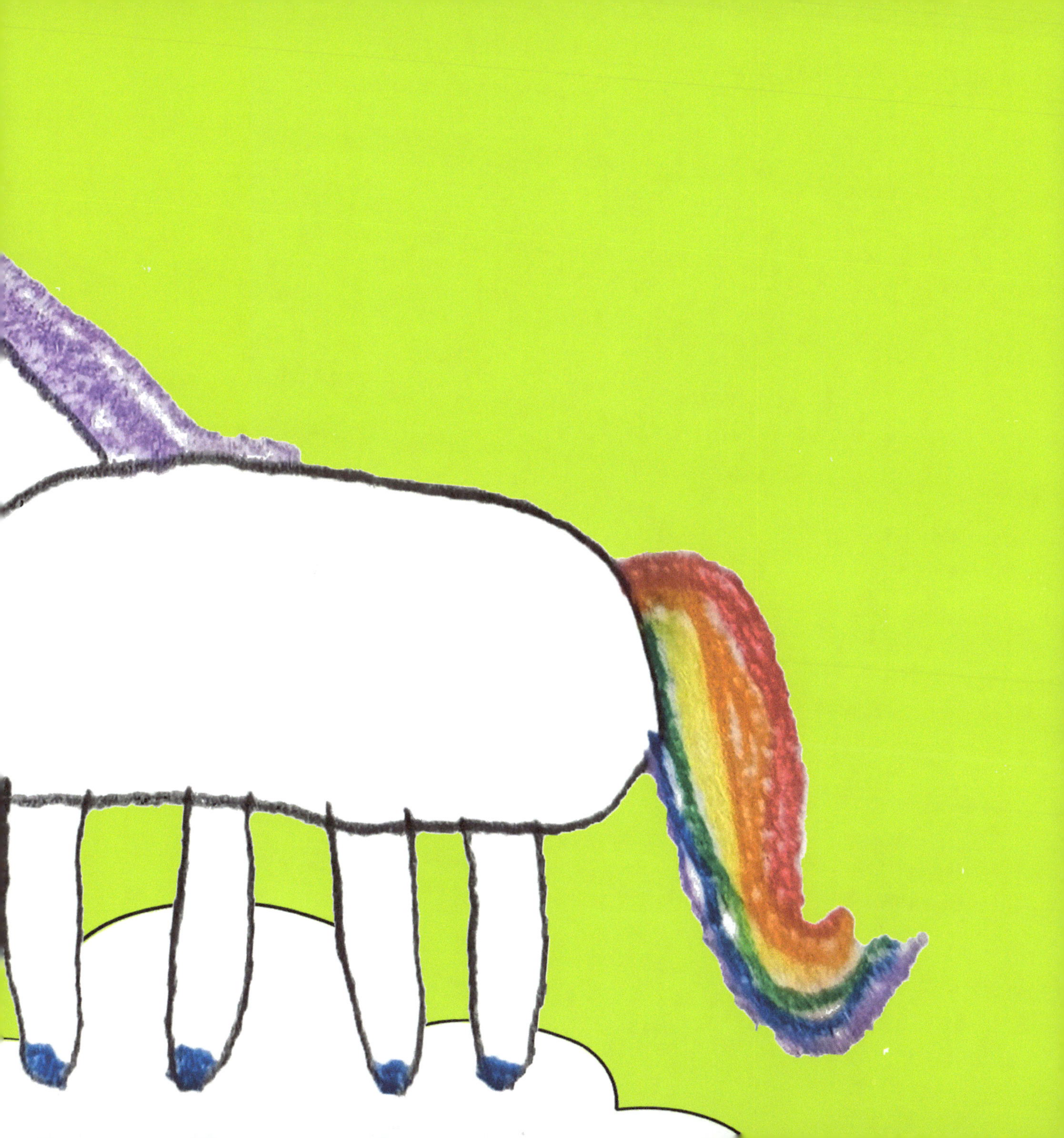

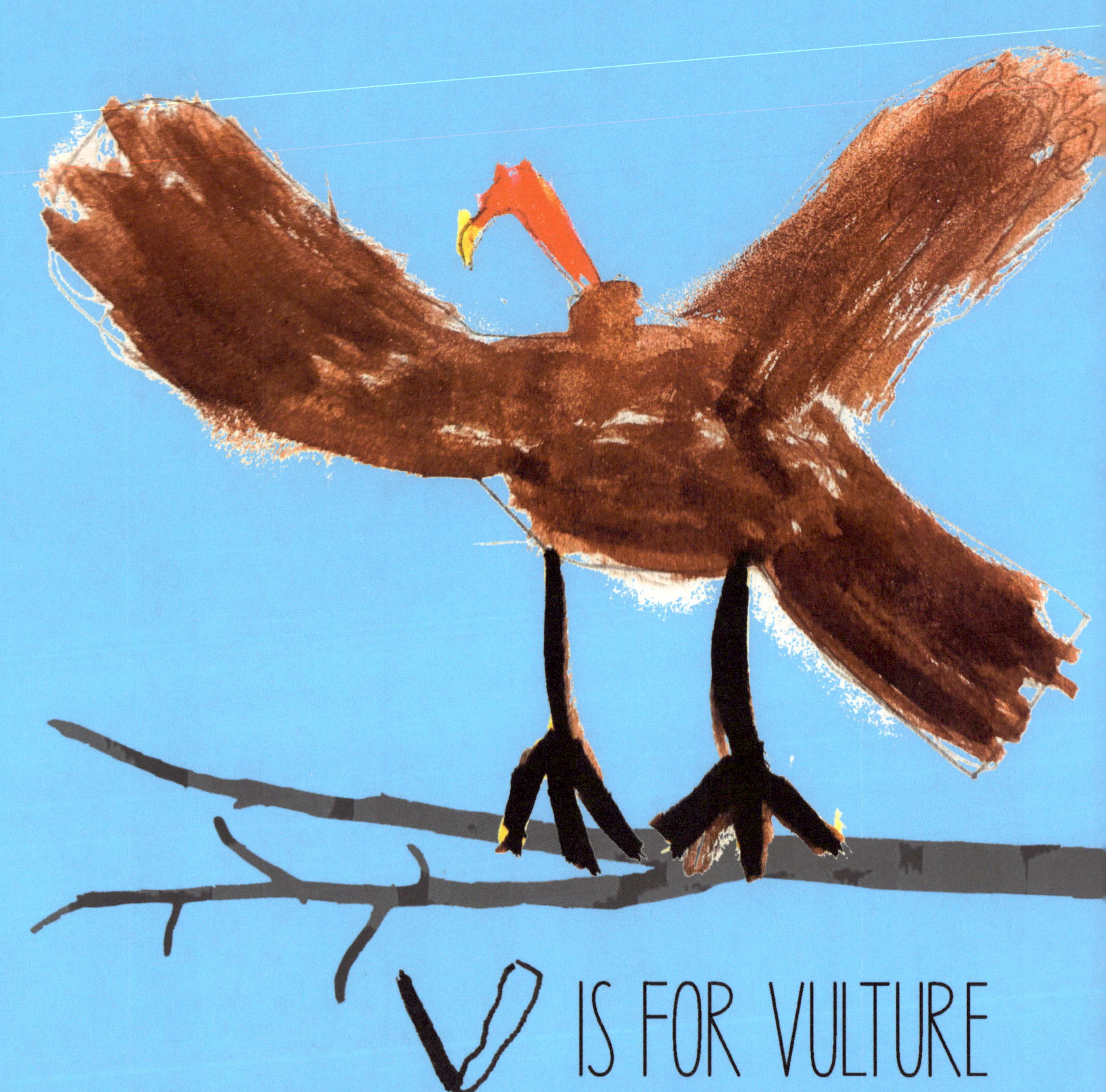
V IS FOR VULTURE

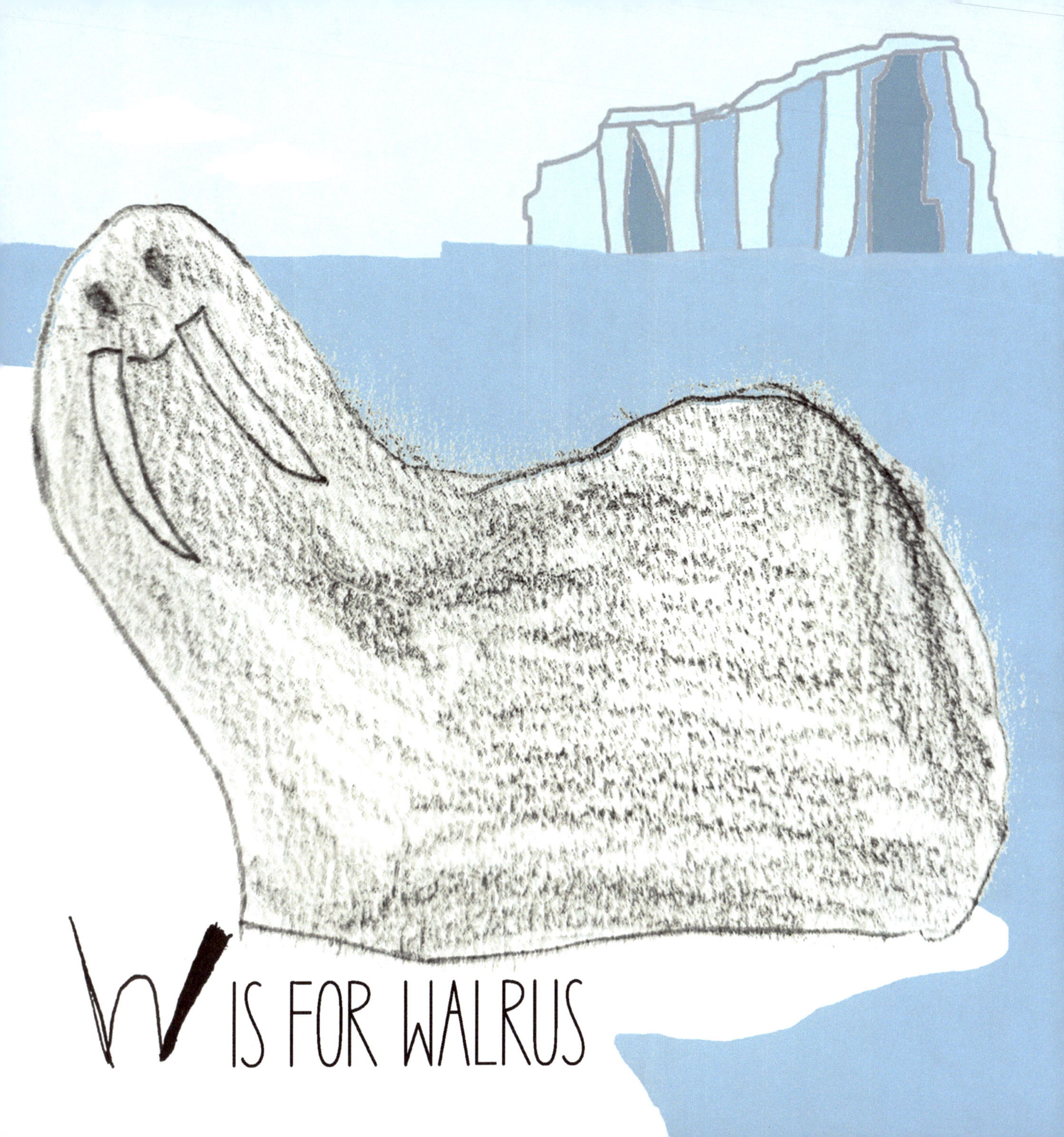

W IS FOR WALRUS

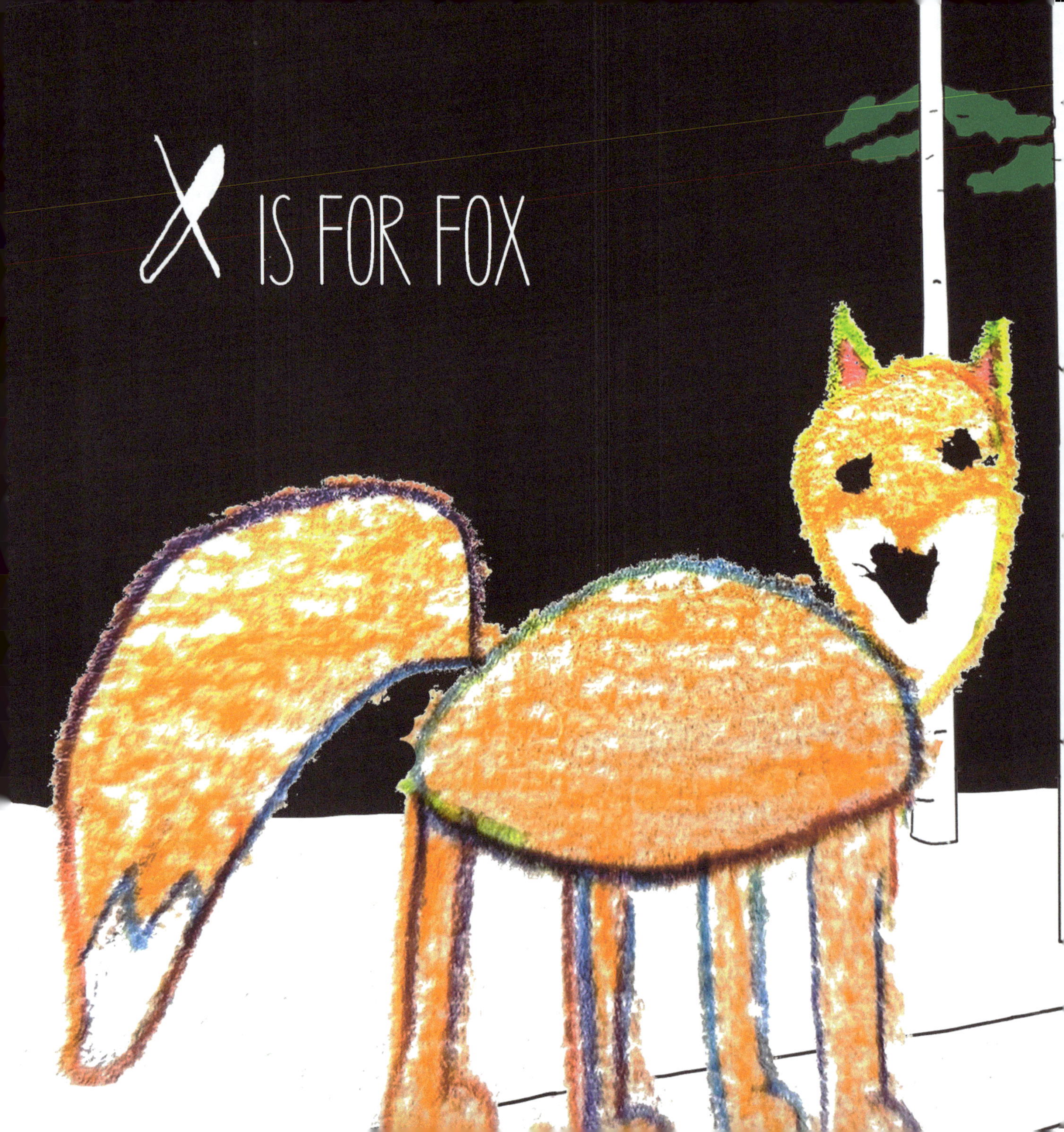
X IS FOR FOX

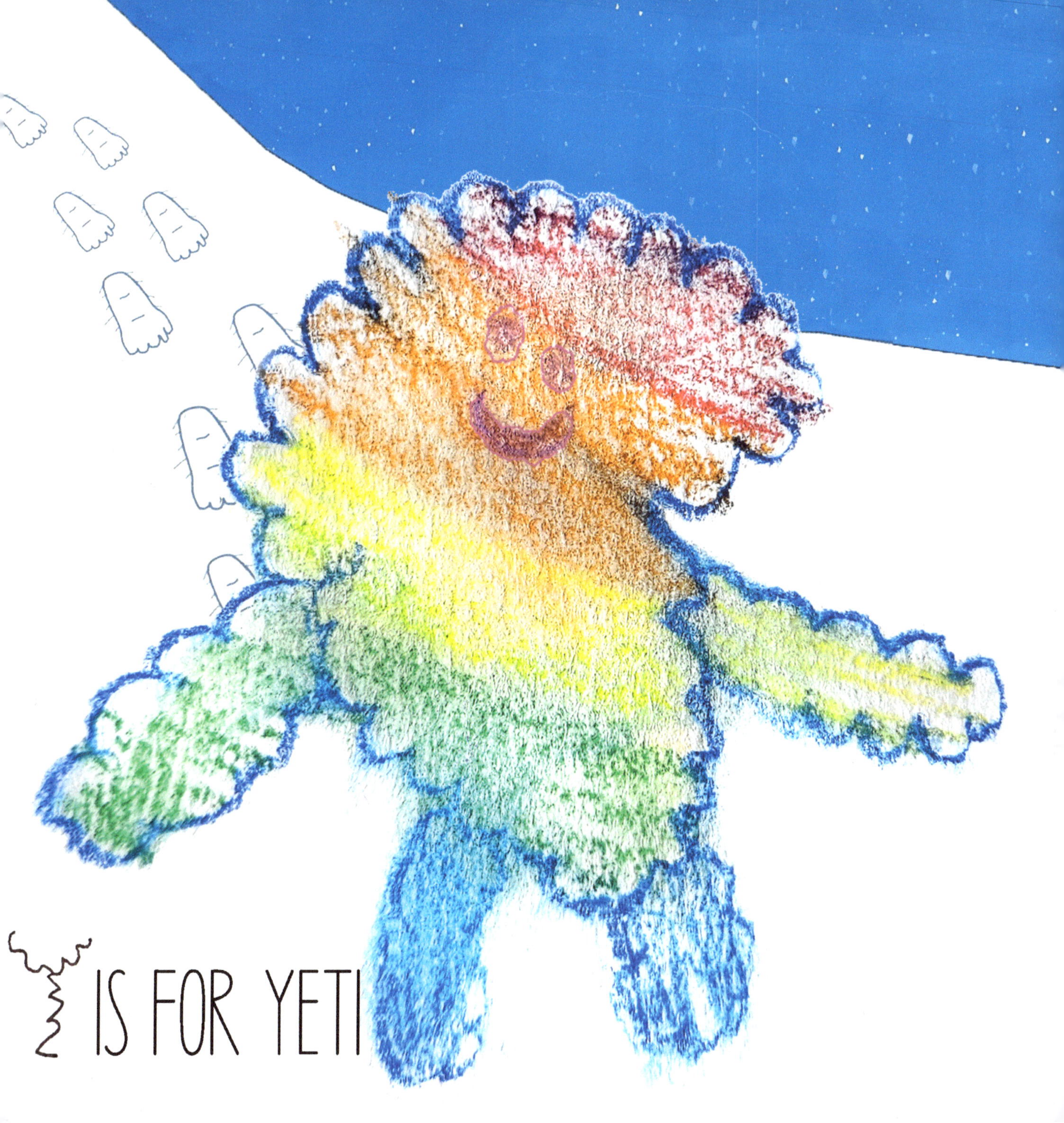
IS FOR YETI

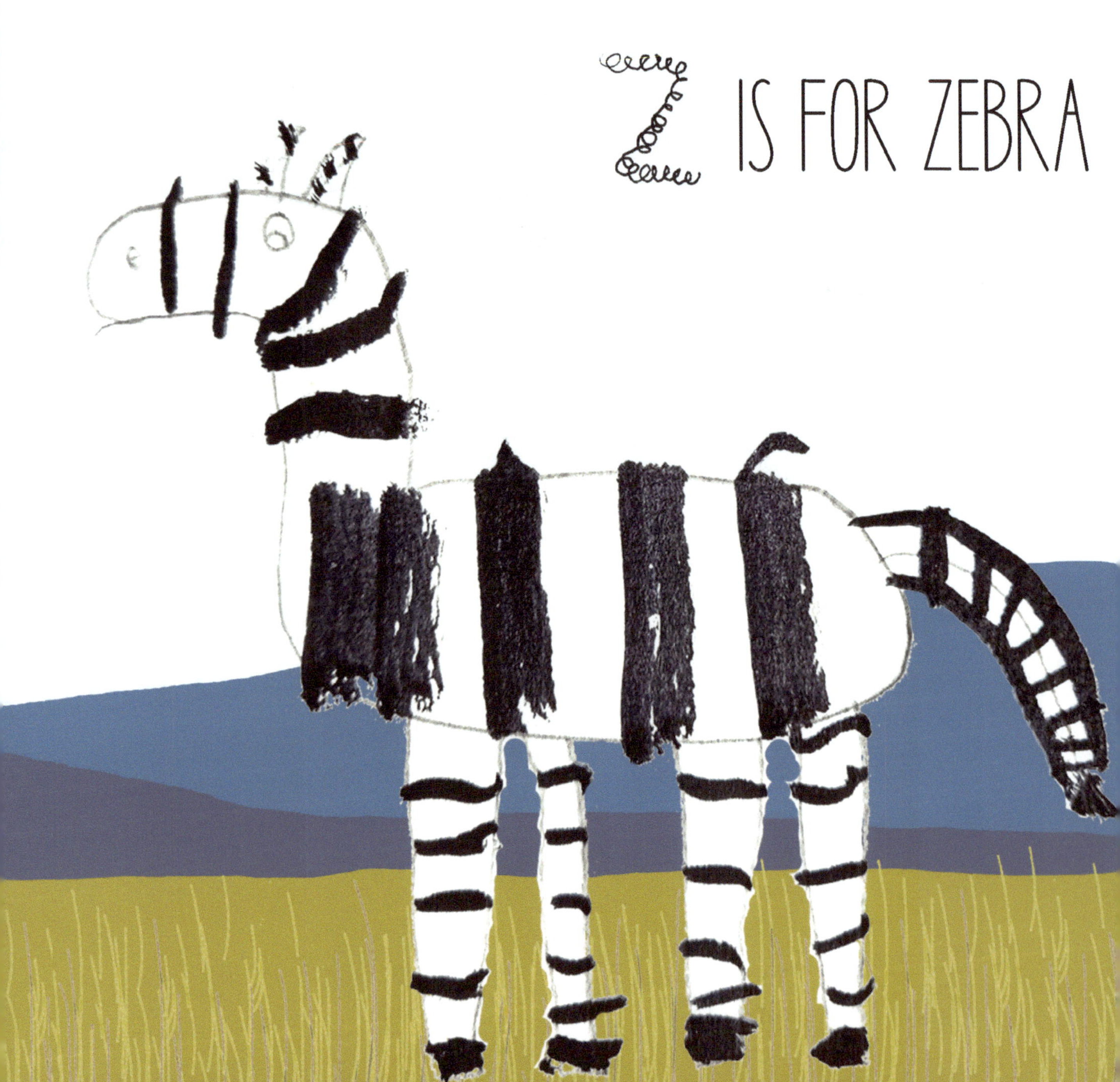

Z IS FOR ZEBRA

ETTA'S ENCHANTING FONT

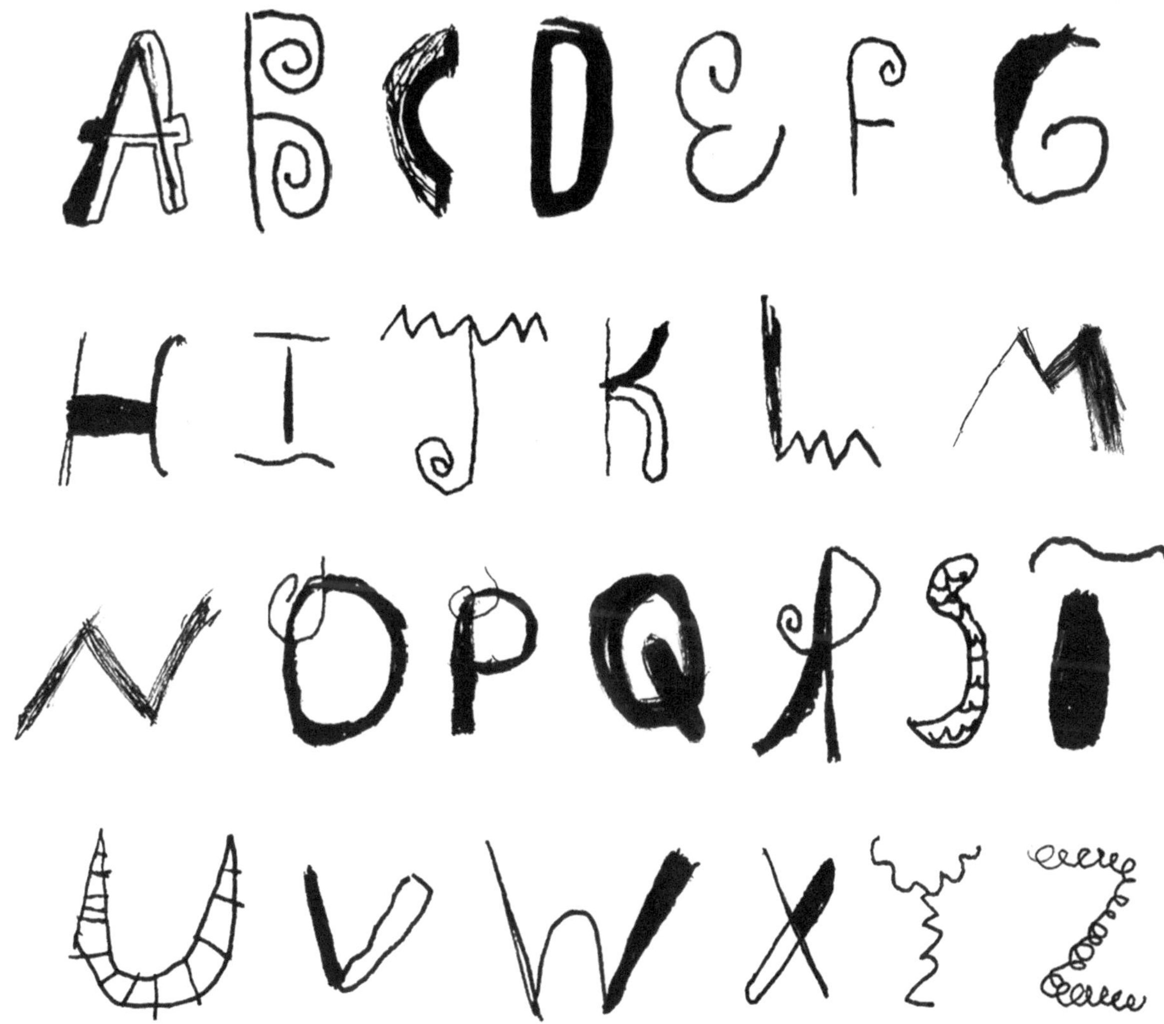

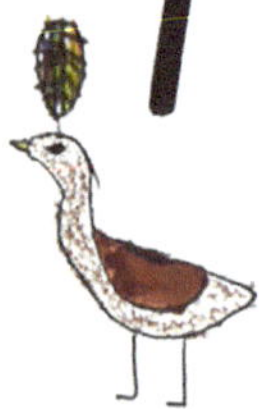

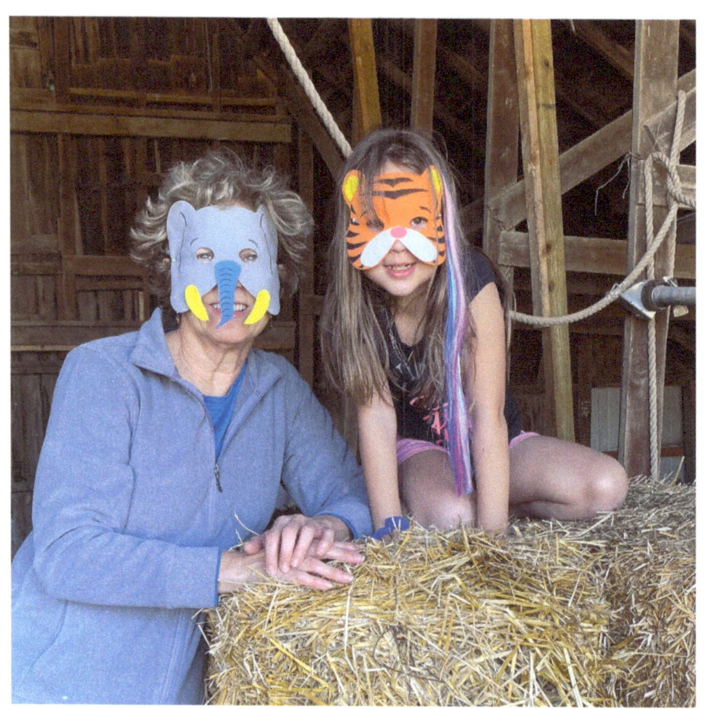

GRANDMA AND ME

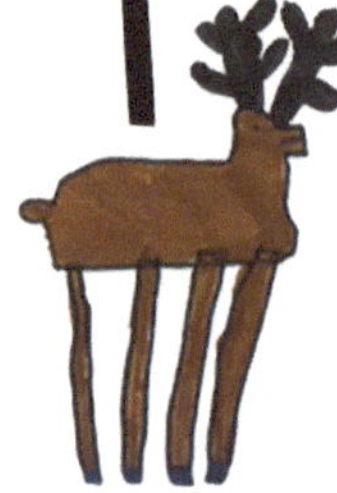

This eye-catching alphabet book can be enjoyed by all ages. It is a warmhearted collaboration between a seven-year-old child named Etta and her grandmother. The book is a collection of 26 animal drawings from A-Z. The animals were illustrated by Etta and the background was added by her grandmother. In addition, a unique alphabet lettering font was created by this young artist.

Drawing at an early age can be imaginative and inventive. Capturing her granddaughter's creative spirit at a tender age was the motivation behind the making of this book. Pablo Picasso said, "Every child is an artist. The problem is how to remain an artist once he grows up."

While teaming up to complete the book, questions unraveled between Etta and her grandmother. A love for working together and sharing each other's ideas helped to create a fun, lasting memory. Grandmas everywhere, enjoy this whimsical book. A childlike perspective makes it an ideal first alphabet book for young minds.

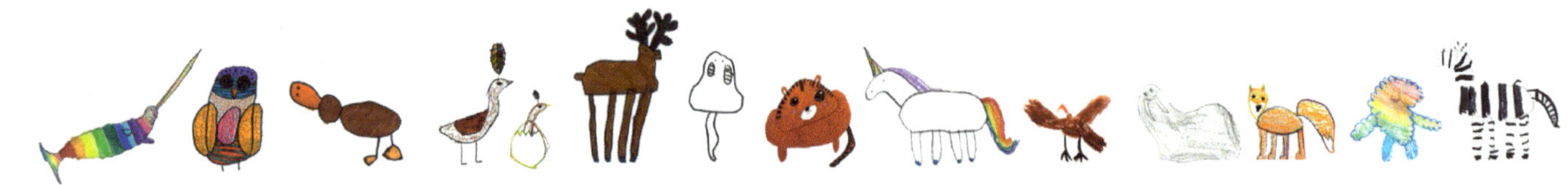

www.ingramcontent.com/pod-product-compliance
Lightning Source LLC
Chambersburg PA
CBHW042023110726
48010CB00007B/215